the beginner's
em@il
book

the beginner's
em@il
book

best practice in setting up
and managing your system

foulsham
LONDON • NEW YORK • TORONTO • SYDNEY

foulsham

The Publishing House, Bennetts Close, Cippenham,
Slough, Berkshire SL1 5AP, England

ISBN 0–572–02674–9

Printed in Great Britain by St. Edmundsbury Press, Bury St. Edmunds, Suffolk

Contents

Introduction

These days it seems everyone communicates by e-mail. Every business, store, television programme, charity, school and community group seems to offer an e-mail address to which you can send comments and from which you can get further information, and the media proclaim the arrival of the 'information age'. If you don't have e-mail, you might be feeling a little left out. But is e-mail really for you? What do you need and how do you get started? This book should help you find out.

How can this book help me?

This book aims to help you find what will work best for you. It suggests ways to 'try before you buy' and find an e-mail solution that suits your own particular requirements. When you are ready to start sending e-mail, it explains how to write, send, receive and reply to messages; how to attach, send and receive files; and how to manage your stored messages. It provides examples of how software features and functions can be used, and looks at some of the other ways in which you can reach and correspond with other e-mail users with whom you may share an interest. It explains jargon and suggests ways to make your messages clearer and more acceptable to other users, and much more.

Is this book right for me?

Read this book if you:

* Use a PC or Macintosh computer at home and would like to use e-mail to keep in contact with friends and family or for working at home.

- Run a small or new business and are considering introducing e-mail for office communication or for website or e-commerce support.

- Work for an organisation that is introducing e-mail, and want to understand what it's all about.

- Don't have a computer or any Internet experience, but want to learn more about e-mail and how to use it. Yes, there are ways to send and receive e-mail without owning a computer at all!

Examples and guidance are provided for basic tasks such as sending and receiving mail, and suggestions are provided for best practice in how to manage and organise messages. This book does not provide itemised step-by-step guidance on how to install or operate particular software packages: your product manuals will explain how to do this, and you should keep them to hand while reading this book to help answer any queries you may have.

In order to use this book you will need to know the basics of computing, such as how to use a keyboard and mouse and how to find items on the screen, but technical jargon is avoided where possible and explained where not. Some frequently used terms are used deliberately, as you will need to become familiar with them. You should be able to find any unfamiliar terms in the glossary at the back of the book.

This book uses Microsoft® Outlook Express e-mail software for most examples, purely for consistency and to avoid confusion between examples from different products. Don't worry if you use another e-mail product: most of the functions are very similar. Some details are provided of the alternative names used by products in common use. If you have a manual for your e-mail software, keep this to hand as you might need to refer to it.

How to use this book

This book contains eight chapters and three appendixes. It starts with a brief history of e-mail, the reasons for using it and the conventions and rules you are expected to follow; works through the basic procedures of sending, receiving and managing your messages; looks at alternative uses for e-mail;

and discusses some of the more advanced features, which are primarily of interest to high-volume or business users. The appendixes provide reference information, such as useful website addresses and details of where to find corresponding functions in different e-mail software. Finally, there is a glossary explaining unusual terms and jargon, and an index to help you locate the information you require within the book.

Throughout this book you will find words shown in italic. These are usually e-mail, Internet or computer terms that may be unfamiliar to you: the italic indicates that they are explained in the glossary at the end of the book. Most terms are shown in italic on their first use only.

Products featured in this book

Throughout this book you will find sample screens and descriptions of features of Microsoft® Outlook Express and MSN™ Hotmail® software. There are also some sample screens, guidance and information provided for other e-mail and Internet software, including Netscape® Messenger™ and QUALCOMM® Eudora®.

These products have been selected because they are in common use at the time of writing and provide a variety of features useful both to the home and business user. As technology advances quickly, more recent versions of this software might be available by the time you read this book, or the version you use on your computer might look somewhat different, especially if you use an operating system other than Windows®. However, the information in this book is not version-specific, so it will still be valid, even if the images on your computer screen look a little different.

Trademarks and registered marks

Several product names mentioned in this book are trademarks of other companies:

- Microsoft, Internet Explorer, Outlook Express, MSN and Hotmail are either registered trademarks or trademarks of the Microsoft Corporation in the United States and most other countries.

- Netscape, Netscape Navigator and the Netscape N logo are registered trademarks of Netscape Communications

CHAPTER 1

What's all the fuss about?

There is a lot of talk these days about the new 'information age', the 'electronic era' and an 'e-mail revolution'. What exactly do these terms mean? In this chapter we look at the recent history of e-mail; where it came from and why it has become so popular, and some of the uses it has both for home and business. Finally we have a quick preview of how e-mail looks, to help allay any fears you may have about its complexity.

The information age

E-mail, or 'electronic mail', developed from the Internet, a visionary system that started as a communications project for the US military in the 1970s and gradually developed into a commercial networking system. When the military handed over control of its system to the private sector in the mid-1990s, the idea of an accessible, non-regulated, world-wide information system was already taking hold of corporate minds. The perceived benefits of online advertising and trading (*e-commerce*), combined with the reducing cost of home and business computing, led to the Internet becoming the international business tool, information provider and leisure organiser we know today.

The Internet basically allows anyone with a PC, modem and suitable software to read information stored on other computers, known as *servers,* which have been linked to the Internet deliberately by their owners. Such owners may include a small, local engineering firm; a national or multinational corporation; a fast-food chain; a rural community; a government department; a charity; a school or university – almost any organisation you can think of – even some individuals.

The information is usually accessed through the *world-wide web (WWW)*, by visiting a website. Websites are collections of documents (*webpages*) that are linked together by *hyperlinks*, allowing you to 'jump' from one page to another without needing to know the file details. Hyperlinks also allow you to jump from one website to another, and to search the Internet for related topics – this is known as *surfing*. Users of the web do not need to worry whether the website they are viewing is local or overseas: the cost of accessing the site is the same wherever it is located. In fact, you may think you are looking at a local website if the address of the company is local, but it could be on almost any computer, anywhere in the world.

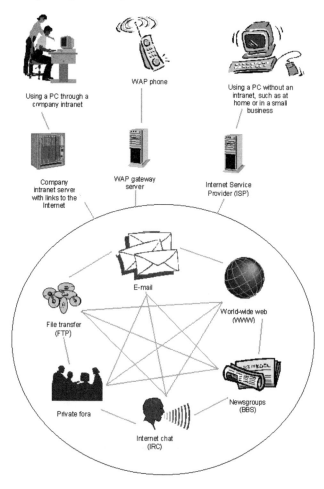

Figure 1: The Internet

There are many other parts to the Internet, including news-groups and bulletin boards, lists, file download sites and online chat facilities, and we shall look at some of these later in the book. Figure 1 shows how the whole network links together. Some of the terms used in this diagram might be unfamiliar, but don't worry, they will be explained later.

The Internet is actually a little more technically complex than this diagram implies: numerous computer systems and satellites support the Internet, allowing links and information flows between computers in various continents. However, Figure 1 gives you a good idea of the types of information you can currently access as an Internet and e-mail user.

E-mail is considered to be part of the Internet because the information is transported via a telephone line and computer servers, and because many organisations with Internet websites use e-mail for communication with their customers: basically if you can access the Internet, you can use e-mail, and vice versa. Most websites have an e-mail facility to allow people visiting the site to send comments, queries or orders directly to the owner.

Research estimates there are around half a billion Internet and e-mail users regularly visiting websites and newsgroups and writing and reading e-mail, and this number is growing exponentially. The information that businesses and other organisations provide on their websites has become as effective a marketing tool as expensive print advertising, with no limit on its audience. Information has therefore become a valuable commodity – hence the term 'information age'.

The e-mail revolution

Basic, text-only electronic mail has been available in one form or another since before the Internet was even considered. The earliest versions of e-mail, in the 1960s, allowed employees within a company to communicate quickly and cheaply, maintaining a written record of discussions. This proved especially popular for large organisations spread over several sites. However, users were restricted to communications within their own company, or occasionally within the organisation providing the service, if this covered more than one company. These providers, including an early incarnation of

CompuServe®, were the forerunners of today's *Internet Service Providers*, or ISPs.

With the vast increase in demand for e-mail in the late 1980s, the providers realised that connection from one system to another was not only desirable, but also inevitable. It was only logical to link up with the development of the Internet. Now most medium and large businesses operate e-mail for internal mail and to receive mail from outside the company (for example from customers and suppliers) and many allow some or all of their employees to send external mail. Small businesses often have a single e-mail address from which they communicate with the outside world. With the cost of e-mail and Internet access falling, the popularity of home computing is increasing – particularly among families now that most schools are equipped with computers – so more and more people now have Internet and e-mail facilities at home. This sudden growth in the market is what is commonly called the 'e-mail revolution'. It has led to what is called the 'electronic era' or 'global village': with business and commerce promoting products via the Internet, goods and services are made available to anyone, anywhere in the world at the touch of a button. It's as if everything in the whole world was available in your local shop.

Why is e-mail so popular?

The ability to send e-mail to any other e-mail user in the world is one of the most important parts of the development of the Internet, certainly for business. It is not surprising that the business community has embraced the facility with such relish:

- E-mail is cheaper than a long telephone call or fax and quicker than a letter.

- E-mail can be sent to more than one location simultaneously. It costs no more to send an e-mail to 50 people than it does to send it to one – in terms of both time and money.

- E-mail is everywhere; more and more businesses are implementing it, so it is ideal for business-to-business communication.

- E-mail can include words, pictures, sounds and video – any kind of computer file – making it ideal for business communications that require supporting visual or audio material.

- E-mail is easy to set up and use and suitable for everyone from the computer novice to the technology expert.

- E-mail is portable: once you have an address, you can usually dial in to read and send mail from almost any computer and modem. You are not restricted to using only your own PC in your own home or office.[1]

As with many other good ideas, e-mail is just as suitable for non-business use in the wider world. Once access to the world-wide web via the Internet became available to all, e-mail was bound to take off for personal and social use. It allows anyone with a PC and modem to communicate with anyone else with a PC and modem, at low cost, even internationally, and can carry not only text but also documents, images, sound and video.

Many people with relatives abroad find e-mail indispensable: it costs only the price of a local phone call at most to send a letter, family pictures, or anything else that you can store on a computer. And with *cybercafés* (sometimes called Internet cafés), computer-enabled public libraries and community facilities becoming more accessible, even those without a PC can get in on the act. I recently received an e-mail message from an Australian friend who was trekking in the Himalayas: she had found a cybercafé in Kathmandu and decided it would be quicker to send an e-mail message than a postcard. A few weeks later, she sent another from Moscow, attaching scanned photographs of her trip. I have since been able to track her progress around the world by an e-mail message every few weeks, each from somewhere new. By mail these 'postcards' would have taken some weeks to arrive and the cost of postage would have been far greater. E-mail is a great way to keep in touch with friends and family around the world, and allows you to communicate with others cheaply and easily – whatever their location.

We will look in more detail at the pros and cons of e-mail in the next chapter.

---

[1] This is not always the case. When using an intranet (a company's internal network) you can usually only log in from a computer within that company, as the company's information will be protected by a firewall to prevent access from anyone outside the company, particularly hackers. However, should you be unable to use the computer on your own desk for some reason, you should still be able to log in from another computer in your company's offices.

Common uses for e-mail

The lists below show some of the ways in which e-mail is most commonly used, both by business and at home:

Business use

- Sending notices of meetings and events to a group of employees.

- Keeping staff informed via e-mailed newsletters and documents.

- Day-to-day communication between team members.

- Sending documents and images to customers and suppliers, for example details of a product range, or instructions for production.

- Obtaining business information, for example, using a newsgroup to keep up with developments on a product range.

- Allowing feedback and enquiries from your company's website.

Personal or social (home) use

- An alternative to letters for friends and family; you can send photos without needing reprints!

- Arranging and publicising events for community and social groups.

- Mass-mailing documents: for example, sending your CV to agencies or employers.

- Making contact and keeping in touch with others of similar interest: for example, via Internet bulletin boards, list services or newsgroups.

- Obtaining further information from Internet websites, usually via a link from that site directly to their e-mail address.

- Generating interest in and feedback/enquiries from your or your community group's website.

What does e-mail look like?

If you are unfamiliar with computers, you might be worried that e-mail will be far too complex for you to understand. Don't worry! E-mail software is designed for all, not just for the computer whiz-kid: it's much easier than programming your VCR. Most e-mail software uses images that you will recognise to identify parts of the system, and this makes it easy to use. For example, a message is often shown as an envelope; a contacts list as an address book; a folder or group of messages as a folder symbol (see the examples on the next few pages). Most software these days comes with extensive online help, even including prompts that appear when you move the mouse pointer over an item on the screen to tell you what it is. Most products also have a printed or online manual containing step-by-step guides to the major functions.

The actual appearance of e-mail depends upon which software you are using, as the examples on the next few pages show:

- Figure 2, from Microsoft® Outlook Express, shows the main window from which you send, receive and manage your messages.

- Figure 3 shows the MSN™ Hotmail® inbox: this is one of the free e-mail sites often used in libraries and cybercafés and by people on the move as it can be accessed from anywhere with an Internet connection. Don't be put off by all the advertising in this window; this is how the creators of MSN™ Hotmail subsidise their free service.

- Figure 4 shows the equivalent in QUALCOMM® Eudora®.

- Figure 5, taken from Netscape® Messenger™, shows the message window in which you type your message and in which a received message would appear.

- Figure 6 shows an example of the online help available in Microsoft® Outlook Express.

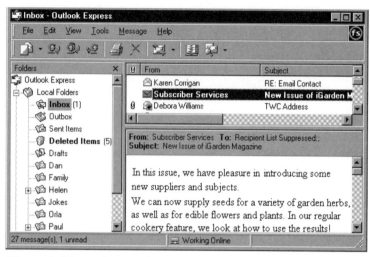

Figure 2: The main e-mail window (Microsoft® Outlook Express)

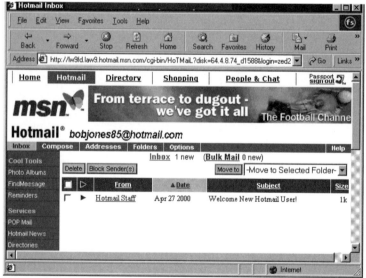

Figure 3: The main e-mail window (MSN™ Hotmail)

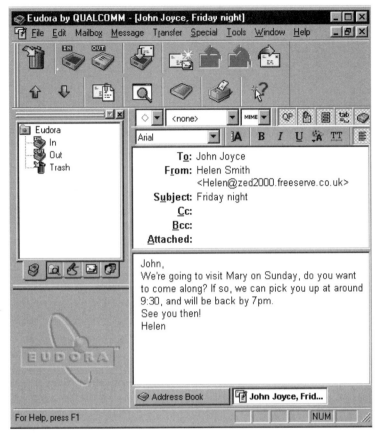

Figure 4: The main e-mail window (QUALCOMM® Eudora®)

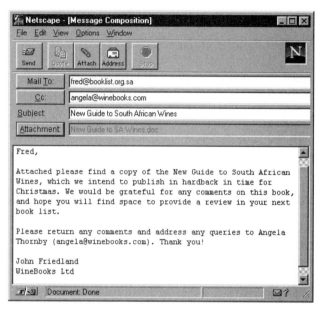

Figure 5: A typical e-mail message (Netscape® Messenger™)

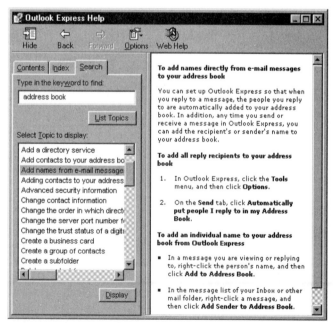

Figure 6: An example of online help (Microsoft® Outlook Express)

Throughout the rest of this book, we use Microsoft® Outlook Express exclusively for examples, to avoid confusion between products. If you use a different program, refer to the appendix *Alternative names for e-mail functions* for details of alternative names for functions and options described in this book. If your product is not listed in the appendix, refer to the user manual or online help that accompanies your product.

CHAPTER 2

Why do I need e-mail?

E-mail is not for everyone, although the media would have us believe that without an e-mail address and a PC with accompanying cables and flashing lights we are out of touch with the modern world. This is just not so. Indeed, there are people to whom e-mail is no great benefit and for whom such investment would be a waste of time and money; there are many others who really don't need e-mail at home or for work, but would occasionally like to fiddle around on the Internet and send a few messages to their friends.

In this chapter, we look at the advantages and disadvantages of e-mail for home and business use, and some ways in which you can try e-mail before deciding whether or not to buy your own system. We look at what you need to use e-mail on your own computer, and finally discuss whether or not you should wait to see how technology develops.

E-mail at work

E-mail was originally designed as a business tool, and it has been rapidly adopted as the replacement for the memo. Indeed, many businesses would now find it difficult to survive without e-mail, so dependent are they upon it as an all-round method of communication. Most commonly, e-mail is used in business for:

- Communicating with established customers.

- Communicating with suppliers.

- Sending documents to staff, customers and suppliers.

- Arranging meetings and sending agenda.

- Sending communiqués to a large number of staff.

- Messages between staff on the company's intranet.

The last item is a double-edged sword for many an employer. E-mail can be the equivalent of the office gossip, only worse, as it is not always possible to tell whether an employee is working or sending a personal message and their audience is far wider. With a few keystrokes, a message can be sent from one employee to another, to several, or to anyone in the company: if the system allows e-mail to be sent and received from outside the company, the employee can send messages and documents to any e-mail user in the world. Therefore there are some disadvantages to e-mail at work:

- Time wasted on gossip and junk e-mail (jokes, chain letters and personal e-conversations).

- Possible breaches of security with documents leaving the company.

- The possibility of legal action being taken over comments written in an e-mail message.

- The possibility of fraud, with unauthorised employees sending orders and confidential documents to suppliers or competitors.

However, all of the above can be minimised if a system is correctly installed with suitable security levels, and if staff are made aware of the expectations of the employer – what is and is not acceptable in e-mail use, for example. The problems described are more likely to occur in medium to large companies, and a good precaution is to have intranet, Internet and e-mail systems installed by professionals who take into account such considerations and build protection into the system. Such protection can include e-mail monitoring on a random or comprehensive basis to discourage, and where necessary prove and act upon, misuse of the facility.

Internet or intranet?

An intranet is basically a company's own Internet, just for staff within its own premises. It allows staff to exchange, store and locate information on a network in the same way they would on the Internet, but with all the security of a self-contained system. Because the network operates between computers within the same location or organisation, there is no additional cost to the business for time spent online, so there is usually no need to dial in, although users will need a user name and password to connect (or *log in*) to the network. There are several advantages to this, but in effect it works in a similar way to the local-area network (LAN) or wide-area network (WAN) used by most large companies to organise and store files and programs for staff use. Like these networks, an intranet is usually designed and installed by professional network consultants, as it is a rather technical business.

One major consideration for most businesses is whether to give their staff access to the Internet. In most cases, the answer is no – the temptation to waste time surfing the Internet instead of working productively is often just too great. However, for some businesses access to the Internet, and with it, access to competitors', suppliers' and customers' websites, is of great benefit. For the larger company it is usually worth considering whether to restrict such access to people who really need it in their day-to-day business, or whether to place restrictions on the types of site that each person is allowed to access. Most reputable Internet/intranet consultants will be able to offer packages of security tailored to your company's needs.

Most smaller companies will not need an intranet, unless staff are spread across several sites and frequently need to exchange information in document form.

E-mail for the small business

Is e-mail really necessary for most small businesses? This really depends on what business you are in, and what you would use e-mail for. As part of a wider implementation of, say, a website or e-commerce facility, e-mail can be vital. If you create a website without the facility for visitors to e-mail you, prospective customers will be less likely to make contact. While you may receive spurious e-mail if you provide an e-mail link from your site, it is likely that you will receive mainly genuine queries, some at least of which could generate revenue.

If you have no plans for a company website, but you are considering e-mail as a method for communicating with customers and suppliers, you should first establish whether such communication would be acceptable to them. See whether they would be more likely to use e-mail than other communication methods for their communication with your company. Some businesses prefer to continue using traditional communication methods, with e-mail used as a back-up or informal messaging system only. Try to gauge whether the introduction of e-mail could result in increased business, and from this decide whether to just offer it as an option or suggest that it become the preferred communication medium. There are several issues here, including the following:

- Because e-mail has indefinite legal status in some areas (see the section *Legal considerations* on page 117), many suppliers will not accept orders or changes to orders via e-mail but only via online forms designed specifically for the purpose.

- Some customers may view e-mail as too informal a method of communication.

- Some of your customers or suppliers might not have the facility to send or receive e-mail.

As a marketing tool, e-mail is not particularly effective. In its basic form it allows little embellishment of text, so provides no visual impact. Remember that any e-mail message will probably arrive in an inbox already crammed with other text messages, and is easily discarded, overlooked or ignored.

A good way to judge the likely effectiveness of introducing e-mail is to look at your direct competitors or similar businesses. Do they use e-mail? If so, what do they use it for? Is it only as part of their website, or for more general communication? Are their clients urged to use e-mail for all transactions, or only for queries? If they don't have e-mail, try to find out why not. Have they tried it and found it ineffective? Or are you simply one step ahead of them all?

Another consideration, especially for the very small business with one or two employees, is the cost of additional telephone lines. If you intend to use e-mail or the Internet regularly, your telephone line will be tied up whenever you are online. In most cases it is worth the expense of installing a second line, unless little of your business is conducted by phone or fax. If you intend to send or receive images or large documents regularly, it is worth considering paying the extra for a high-speed digital line or even an *ISDN* connection; otherwise it can take a very long time to receive such documents.

Finally, the most important consideration is whether you have the time to answer your e-mail. There are few things more irritating to the e-mail or Internet user than a person or company that does not respond to an e-mail message. This seems to be a particular problem with e-mail sent using an e-mail link from a website, often requesting more information. If a prospective customer, after viewing your website or an advertisement containing your e-mail address, sends you a request for information and you do not answer it within 48 hours, you are likely never to hear from them again. The sender is likely to think that the message did not get through, the address is no longer used or the company is no longer in business, or that you are too busy to answer the query and therefore too busy to handle their possible order.

E-mail at home

Why would you want e-mail at home? Well, most people do not purchase a computer specifically with e-mail in mind; more commonly their first use of e-mail is via the Internet, when requesting information using a link from a website. But as the use of e-mail spreads, it is becoming an alternative to the telephone and written letter for many people, especially those with family or friends in far-flung locations. The relative cost of sending an e-mail, which can contain text and pictures, compared with the cost of an airmailed letter or, worse, an international telephone call, is a major attraction. For some, it costs nothing; for others, just the cost of a local call; at worst, the cost of a national call. (See the section *Choosing a service provider* on page 30 for more details on the cost of e-mail.) In addition, you can send one message to any number of people without incurring extra cost – great news for the reluctant letter-writer!

The actual benefit depends on how many of your friends and family have access to e-mail. If none of them is online at home or work, or interested enough to use the Internet at a library or cybercafé, you are wasting your time. On the other hand, if you want to make new contacts via the Internet it is essential to have e-mail – often a basic facility will suffice, such as that offered by the free e-mail sites on the Internet.

E-mail, in combination with the Internet, is great for people with hobbies or unusual interests. You can seek out others of similar interests on the Internet, then communicate with them via e-mail messages. E-mail, of course, is totally faceless communication and ideal for the chronically shy; you need give no details of your name, address or location in your e-mail address, and in theory could pretend to be someone else entirely. Therein lies a warning.

Try before you buy

It is possible to send and receive e-mail even if you do not have a computer of your own. These days, computers with Internet connections are available for you to use in many places, including:

- Cybercafés.

- Libraries.

- Schools and universities.

- Community, social and youth clubs.

- Shopping centres or malls.

- Even pubs!

These are generally available to anyone, although you will probably have to pay a small fee and might need to book in advance or to be a member of the organisation in some cases. Most places charge on an hourly basis, to cover the cost of telephone usage, so if you are using the Internet or e-mail regularly, shop around for the best prices. In places where telephone usage is free for Internet purposes, you might not have to pay, although you might still need to book.

If you have access to one of these computers, you can connect to one of the Internet websites that offer free e-mail addresses (known as *online service providers*, or *OSPs*) and start e-mailing almost immediately. Some of the addresses of the best known OSPs are shown in the appendix *Useful Internet addresses*. Some of these are available world-wide (MSN™ Hotmail® is probably the one in most common use); others are designed for use within a specific country and contain links to Internet sites of local interest to that country. You may find a locally based site more useful, especially if English is not your native language. From these sites you create your own e-mail address and send and receive e-mail. This works rather like an old-fashioned accommodation address – somewhere you can pick up your mail – except that you don't have to pay (other than any charges described above). The OSPs make their money from the advertising that appears on their pages; it can be a little distracting to start with, but you soon get used to it. Obviously the idea is that you follow the advertisers' links and purchase items, but there is no obligation to do so. If you find the advertising intrusive, there is often a way to switch off the display of graphics.

Using shared facilities like this is a good way to try out the Internet and e-mail, to see if it is for you, before deciding whether to invest in equipment of your own. In most of these places there is someone available to give free advice on using the equipment, which is always useful but especially so if you have no prior experience with e-mail or the Internet. Some facilities might also provide short training courses, although you will probably have to pay for these.

There are currently all sorts of new e-mail products coming on to the market, such as TV/PC, PC/TV, and WAP telephones (see *The next big thing* on page 33). Unfortunately there is currently no comparable way to try these before you buy, although some retailers may give you a limited period of test use in-store, or offer you a refund if you are unhappy with a purchase. However, most of these items will offer a less detailed, less functional version of the computer-based e-mail and Internet system, so if you can get along with e-mail on a PC, the alternatives should be easy to master. Whether you prefer to use a large-screen PC or double-function set, or a small hand-held screen that doubles as a phone, is of course up to you.

Buying into e-mail

In this section we look at the equipment and software you need if you want to use e-mail from home or your own office. Here we assume you require a standard computer-based set-up, rather than a wireless or portable solution.

What you need

To send and receive e-mail you need the following:

- A suitable computer with a modem, to allow you to send the electronic message files across the telephone network.

- Connection software, which converts your typed message into a format that can be sent via the modem, and also provides you with an e-mail address, storage on a remote server for messages, and access to the Internet. This software is provided by an ISP; some may be pre-installed on your computer. Even if you intend to use one of the free e-mail services provided on the Internet, you will still require the services of an ISP to connect to the Internet using your telephone line.

- E-mail software, to allow you to type and send, receive and read messages, and, usually, to file them in a structured way. One or more such applications may be pre-installed if you have a recently-purchased computer. Alternatively, you can sign up to an OSP and use their software via the Internet.

Choosing a suitable computer and modem

Most computers for home and office are supplied with a modem already installed. The latest models have modems allowing the fastest connection (currently 56Kbps in most countries); if purchasing a second-hand model, try to find one with a modem speed not less than 28.8Kbps or you will find it time-consuming and costly to send and download messages. If you already have a computer but it does not contain a modem, you should be able to find a suitable model that will attach to your computer, either internally or as a plug-in device. Contact a computer dealer or superstore for details, as this is a technical area outside the scope of this book.

Whatever the speed of your modem, you will always be limited by the quality and speed of your telephone connection. If you intend to use e-mail or the Internet quite heavily, and require a fast connection, it is worth discussing with your telecommunications provider (the company to which you pay your telephone bill) what alternative lines are available. Digital lines provide the best response for general use; if your online work is time-sensitive, or if you will be sending a lot of large documents or images, you may need an ISDN line. If you regularly use the Internet from a standard line but find downloading very slow, an accelerator product might be useful: these can improve the rate at which items are fetched and downloaded from the Internet but have little effect on e-mail. Such products include NetSonic (www.web3000.com) and Download Accelerator (www.downloadaccelerator.com).

Choosing a service provider

An ISP (Internet Service Provider) provides you with, amongst other things, connection software that converts your written e-mail message to a format suitable for transmission down a telephone line and routes it through to its destination. The software also allows you to access and work with the many other facilities available on the Internet.

Connection software used to be expensive to purchase and operate. Now, many ISPs are giving away the software for free – so anxious are they to get people on to the Internet. You will find this software arriving, unsolicited, through the post and being given away in supermarkets, newsagents and petrol stations – in fact almost anywhere. If you already have ISP software and are being charged a fee for using it in addition to call charges, it is time to look around for another supplier. In general, all ISPs offer software with very similar functionality, so for the average user there is little to differentiate between them other than price and service, although there may be some packages that are more suitable for heavy or occasional use, depending on the cost of calls at your location. For the business user, some consideration should be given to the levels of security, amount of storage space, and quality of service offered by an ISP before signing up. For large businesses implementing an intranet, it is recommended that the advice of a professional Internet consultant be sought before a decision is made, to prevent possible data exposure and security problems: cheapest is rarely best in this situation.

As a personal or small business user, there are countless ISPs from which you can choose, each offering a different package. Depending on where you live, you might be able to find an ISP that offers free subscription, free software and free telephone usage, or you might have to pay for one or all of them. For example, in most areas of the United States local telephone calls are free, so ISPs provide local numbers to allow users to surf the net all day without charge. In the UK, most Internet users have to pay for their telephone usage at local rates, but get free software and no monthly charges, or a monthly charge that includes the cost of a certain number of calls, although free calls are set to become the norm in the next few years to boost the UK's Internet usage. In other countries, where use of the Internet and e-mail is less widespread, you might be required to pay a monthly subscription to your ISP in addition to telephone costs. At the time of writing, some countries, such as New Zealand, are experiencing legal wrangles between the telecom companies and ISPs over who is allowed to provide free Internet access and where: despite the power wielded by the telecom operators it seems likely that the result will be free access for more customers, whatever their location.

The best advice is to shop around. In most countries you can now obtain ISP software almost anywhere. Look at several free or trial versions, and assess not just the cost of each, but also the quality and speed of service, and any restrictions. If you sign up with an ISP and find the service or the speed of connection is not good enough, just switch to another. Beware of monthly charges, or of any ISP that requires you to enter credit card details before allowing you access; you might find you are locked into a contract with that ISP, and if you wish to change to another you may have to pay the equivalent of the monthly subscriptions for the remainder of the contract (often up to 12 months). It is not unknown for it to take several weeks of constant calling to get through to an ISP's helpline to arrange termination of a payment agreement. If you are new to computing, beware of ISPs who offer free connection and service but require you to pay for telephone assistance or advice, often at premium rates: unless you are technical or have computer-literate friends, this could cost you dearly if you frequently have problems with your Internet or e-mail programs.

Don't be shy. If you know others who use e-mail or the Internet, ask them who their service provider is, and whether or not they are happy with them. Use the suggestions in *Try before you buy* on page 27 to sample the software from different ISPs without cluttering up your own PC. Some website addresses of ISPs, and of ISP lists provided by third parties, are given in the appendix *Useful Internet addresses*, starting on page 127.

Choosing software

Not only are there numerous service providers, but there is also a wide variety of e-mail software on offer. At the time of writing, the most commonly-used products in most countries are Microsoft® Outlook Express and Netscape® Messenger™ (part of Netscape® Communicator™), because most new home and business computers have this software installed as standard: this might change in the next few years due to recent rulings in the US courts over Microsoft®'s domination of the PC and Internet markets. Many large companies use Lotus Notes®, particularly if they use other Lotus® office products, but this is less common among home or small business users. CompuServe® was for many years the staple communication tool of the financial industry and worked somewhat differently from the usual *browser*, but is now available for more general use and offers easy-to-use e-mail and browser functions. For those on the move who require only basic e-mail facilities, one of the online service providers (OSPs), such as MSN™ Hotmail®, often provides the best solution, as you can sign in from anywhere without requiring details of your server or connection software provided by a specific ISP; as long as you can connect to the Internet somehow, only a user name and password are required.

There are many free trial versions of e-mail software available on the Internet, often providing a limited set of functions or carrying advertising as a subsidy, with the full version being available at a cost. If you can ignore the constantly flashing advertising banners, and don't mind that it may slow things down somewhat, this is a great way to find an e-mail program and Internet browser that really suits you.

It makes little difference which software you use if you only want to send basic messages and attachments. The recipient of your message can use any e-mail application to read your message, and you can receive and read messages from any other e-mail application. The only exception to this is if you are using advanced security features that are only available with specific products, such as digital certificates (this is discussed further in the chapter *E-mail allsorts*, starting on page 105).

Because there is such a wide choice of software available, this book cannot provide details or examples from each one. I could show examples and give instructions for more than one product, but this would probably confuse rather than inform. Where possible, I have tried to describe products and features in more generalised terms, so that the information is valid whatever application you happen to be using at the time, and use Microsoft® Outlook Express to show examples of how such features can be used to solve particular problems. If you are unable to find a feature in your application that is described in this book, consult the online help or user manual for that product and read it in conjunction with this book. Not all features are available in all products; some have different names or a subset of the function described here. Some of the most common products are listed in the appendix *Alternative names for e-mail functions* on page 131, together with the names they use for the functions described in this book.

The next big thing

Technology advances so fast these days that information is almost obsolete before it is written. No doubt in a few years, this book will be the equivalent of a telex or minitel operator's manual today. So should you invest money in today's e-mail technology or wait and see what develops? Let's look at some of the innovations currently being proposed as the new communication solutions.

Currently there is a lot of talk about *WAP* technology. WAP is an acronym for Wireless Application Protocol. This is an exciting new development that allows manufacturers to develop equipment for use with the Internet that is entirely portable, without requiring a wire to connect to the phone line or computer. Soon you will be able to access selected areas of the Internet from a wristwatch. Already you can access a limited amount of Internet-based information from certain mobile phones, and can send and receive your e-mail the same way. While this is certainly useful, it will probably not replace the computer as the primary source of e-mail: it may be handy to send a quick e-mail via your phone during a meeting or look up your favourite Internet sites on the train home, but trying to read text from such a tiny screen will be uncomfortable for more than a few minutes at a time, and writing long messages or viewing e-mail attachments will be even more difficult. It is more likely that the WAP phone will come to be the portable equivalent of e-mail, in the same way that the mobile phone has not totally replaced the traditional landline. One problem with this is that if you receive e-mail from a number of devices, you will be unable to file them efficiently in a single source.

Other manufacturers are concentrating on the television set as a route to the Internet; new digital technology allows you to combine the use of PC and TV in a single unit. Again, access to the Internet and e-mail functions are on offer. This might be more of a threat to the home-use PC market, especially for single people or those with little space to accommodate two separate units. For the family it is less likely to be the main source of either TV or Internet – imagine the family arguments over what to watch! – but it might come to replace the second TV in many homes and could be ideal for the teenager's bedroom. It might also prove popular with the small business, especially individuals working from home who require Internet and e-mail services but do not use a PC for other purposes such as word processing; and is ideal for installation in places such as hotels, where providing TV and Internet access could be a definite marketing advantage.

Other manufacturers are combining a keyboard and small screen into a household telephone, to allow a multipurpose communication device. This is likely to capture a small market, like the TV/PC described above. Others, mostly computer manufacturers, are combating the TV/PC with PC/TV: television from your computer, rather than the other way around. This will allow you to view television from your computer, maintaining all its other functionality, so you can watch your favourite soap while typing your office correspondence, sending your e-mail or surfing the Internet. Unfortunately, unless you have a very recent computer, you will probably still need to purchase a new model, as most existing computers designed for home or small business use do not have the capacity to deal with real-time TV via a phone line.

Another possible development is the network computer (NC). This is a very basic computer comprising just a keyboard and screen, which plugs into your telephone line and gives you access to the Internet and e-mail without any other computing facilities, with storage being provided online for any files you wish to save. Its main advantage is price: when it becomes available it should cost less than half of the price of a portable TV – much less than any Internet-enabled PC available today.

However, the rapid decrease in the cost of all computers may well reduce the need for this product.

It might seem that the PC itself will soon be obsolete, replaced by more portable alternatives, and is not worth purchasing. This is not the case. For occasional users who wish to send and receive text messages only, the TV and PC product combinations may be a viable alternative, but not for business. Certainly computers will become more user-friendly, with less dependence on keyboard entry and complicated dial-up procedures, and faster response from servers, but large businesses in particular are not always at the leading edge of technology when it comes to their own staff equipment. It costs too much to update large quantities of computer hardware every time there is a new development, and the Internet and e-mail are not their sole uses for such equipment, so most businesses are unlikely to trash them without a viable alternative. Large businesses may well invest in WAP phones, and WAP technology in general, but they are unlikely to do away with their desktop and laptop computers, especially if faster access is on offer, as is expected with the introduction of more widespread digital communication and improved landline technology. This includes the implementation and use of fibre optic technology and enhanced broadband services, which are currently being introduced in many countries and which offer both a massive improvement in connection speeds over standard telephone lines and the ability to use one line for many purposes simultaneously.

If the cost of computer equipment is prohibitive, consider using a shared facility, as described in *Try before you buy* on page 27, rather than investing in a computer immediately. You can certainly manage a small part-time business or your personal correspondence with family and friends without needing a computer at home. If you do want to buy, find the highest specification equipment that you can afford to get the longest life from your computer, and use some of the pre-installed e-mail software rather than forking out for software with additional functions immediately. Upgrades to pre-installed software are often available free of charge or at reduced cost from the manufacturer's website. If you can't get on with the software supplied, try some of the trial versions on the Internet until you find one you like better.

Don't be put off by the pace of technology as it's never going to stop or slow down: if you wait three years and then buy a computer it will be more advanced, but will still depreciate just as quickly, so you might as well buy it now!

CHAPTER 3

The basics of e-mail

So you have decided to give e-mail a try. Whether using your own computer at home or work, or paying for time on a shared facility, there are a few things you need to know before you get started.

In this chapter we look at how to get an e-mail address and what it does; some basic rules of etiquette on the Internet that help to ensure you don't offend other e-mail users; some considerations for making your system secure; and other issues that you should think about before you go any further.

All about e-mail addresses

In this section we look at e-mail addresses, the unique identifiers that each e-mail user must have in order to send and receive mail. We shall look at what they are, how they are used, and how to get one and how to let others know what it is.

What is an e-mail address?

E-mail addresses are the electronic equivalent of the 'pigeon holes' that used to be in every office mailroom. Each person or department of a business has a unique address, which looks something like this:

    fred@british-computers.co.uk
    sandra_watts@aol.com
    personnel@microwork.net

The first part of the address (before the @ symbol) usually shows an individual's or department's name; the second part – called the *domain* – contains the company's name, or the name of the service provider (ISP or OSP) if it is a personal e-mail account. There is no legal restriction on what words or names you use in the first part, although you cannot use a name that already exists and you might be unable to use certain characters or character combinations (as explained later in this chapter). Some older providers use numbers instead of names, for example:

10846.253@oldpro.com

The domain name is usually set by the service provider, unless you are operating your own server (usually for business only). There are several conventions for this part of the address, and these are described in the appendix *Abbreviations and codes*, starting on page 121.

The portable communication solution

An e-mail address is not fixed to a physical location: it provides, in theory at least, totally portable communication. You might have to provide details of your usual mail address and your computer equipment when you first request an e-mail address, but this is for security only. It does not mean that you cannot use your address to send and receive mail from another computer. However, if you do so you might need to provide some details for your service provider, such as server names, unless you are using an OSP service designed for access anywhere in the world.

The only reason you need to provide your address and telephone number when you first obtain an e-mail account is so the service provider has a record for its own purposes and knows how to get hold of you in case of any query that cannot be resolved by e-mail. Most service providers will refuse to allocate an e-mail address unless you do provide a contact address and telephone number. This is primarily to avoid abuse of the system by criminals, and in some countries is it enforced by law. To what degree such information is checked and validated depends on which service provider you use, and in which country it is based. Some service providers might pass the contact information to third parties as part of a mailing list, but in many countries legislation on data protection allows you to request that they not do so, and many service providers include a place for you to indicate this on their sign-up pages.

How does it work?

The e-mail address is used by the e-mail and Internet software to route a message through the network. Just like a postal address on a traditional letter, the end of the address is looked at first; it identifies either the country in which the account is based, or the type of organisation (for details, see the appendix *Abbreviations and codes*). From this, and the other information in the second part of the address, the correct *server* and *account* can be located and the message sent there. The information is held there until the specific addressee named in the first part of the e-mail address asks to receive mail. (This is a rather simplistic version of events – the text version of the address and the message gets translated into numeric then binary format and is sent as such – but if you really want the full technical details, you're reading the wrong book and are way ahead of us already!)

For example, Bob Jones (bob_jones@isp.co.uk), who lives in London, UK, writes a message to his brother John in Brisbane, Australia, whose e-mail address is john@reeftours.co.au When Bob sends the message, it goes first to the e-mail server operated by his service provider, or to his company's server if he were working on an intranet. Once the transfer of the message to the server is complete, Bob can disconnect (sometimes referred to as *logging out* or *logging off*), ending the call and saving on phone costs. On arrival at the server, the message is examined, and the location determined. The message is then routed to Australia in the same way as an international phone call, but without Bob incurring the cost. The receiving server in Australia routes the mail to the appropriate server for the company Reeftours, and John receives the message when he next connects to the server or refreshes his mailbox.

All this routing can be traced via the technical information in the e-mail header. This is normally hidden from view as it is rather meaningless and off-putting to the average user, but if you want to find the information for a specific message, it is usually available to view. For more information on message headers, including how to display them and what some of the items mean, see *The messsage header* on page 113.

Getting an e-mail address

If you are using e-mail at work, you will probably be given a specific address that is consistent with others in the organisation. If you run your own business, or use e-mail for personal business, you can create your own when you subscribe to the Internet using an ISP. If you are using a shared facility, such as those available at libraries, universities or cybercafés, you can get an e-mail address by filling in an online form for an online service provider (OSP) at a free e-mail site – details of some of the most popular of these are provided in the appendix *Useful Internet addresses*. ISPs and OSPs are referred to in the rest of this book as service providers where the information is applicable to both.

There are millions of individuals and companies world-wide who already have e-mail addresses and the Internet will not allow any name to be duplicated, so you might find that you have to try several alternatives before your choice is accepted. This is particularly likely if you are using your own name and have a common surname, and especially if you are using a service that is available world-wide, such as the OSPs on the Internet or some of the larger ISPs such as AOL or CompuServe®. You can usually get around this by altering the format slightly; for example, if Bob Jones was unable to call himself bob_jones@isp.co.uk because another user was already using that address, he could try one of the following:

    bobjones@isp.co.uk
    bob.jones@isp.co.uk
    b_jones@isp.co.uk
    jones_bob@isp.co.uk
    bob_j@isp.co.uk

Some service providers will actually suggest alternatives for you if your selected name is already in use, usually involving the addition of a counter on the end of your selected name (this indicates the number of people already using that name). It might be a little demoralising to find you are the 3,624th Bob Jones to sign up, but you can always try other alternatives. As it is fairly easy for most of us to forget or mistype numbers, you might prefer to use a nickname to avoid the need for numbers in your address. Beware of using jokey names unless you have a separate address for business: it might be all right to use flufftail@hotmail.com or partyanimal@isp.co.uk for personal friends, but it would raise an eyebrow or two at work.

There are certain characters that cannot be used in any e-mail address. For example, you cannot insert an @ sign except to divide the first part of the address from the second; hash, question and exclamation marks (#, ?, and !) are also forbidden as these symbols are used in programming to mean other things. Avoid the use of accented characters because you cannot key these characters easily on computers in all countries; different languages often mean different keyboard layouts. Some service providers have their own exclusions: for example, some will not allow you to use a dot within the first part of the address, others will. Check with your own service provider if you wish to use a symbol that your software will not accept. In general it is best to stick to combinations of letters, numbers and the underscore character (_), as these are accepted as valid by all systems, appear correctly on computers using foreign language software and are easy to find on foreign keyboards.

Finding other e-mail addresses

In general you must know a person's e-mail address before you can consider sending them a message. Currently there are few e-mail directories in which you could reliably find a person's e-mail address. There are several such facilities advertised on the Internet, but they are either provided by specific service providers or rely on a person having specifically requested an entry in the directory – rather like the *Yellow Pages*. Usually an service provider's own website lists only people who have accounts with that provider and who have consented to allow their details to be used.

However, if you have lost someone's e-mail address these sites offer a good starting point, especially if you can remember which service provider the person uses. Most web *search engines* and service provider websites provide a 'people search' option, in which you can enter a person's first and last name and other details such as address, postcode and company, to try to locate further details. Some examples are given in the appendix *Useful Internet addresses*, starting on page 127.

Some service providers automatically include you in their own directories, although you should always be given the option not to be listed. For example, if you set up an e-mail account with MSN™ Hotmail® (www.hotmail.com) they will offer to put your address in the Internet White Pages and the Hotmail® directory. Whether or not you do so is a matter of personal choice (see below).

Allowing others to find you

There's no point having an e-mail address if nobody knows what it is. The best way to make sure your friends and family know your new e-mail address is to send them an e-mail message. That way, they have the address available on their computer, and can reply directly to you. Most e-mail software will allow recipients of your e-mail to add your details to an address book, so they do not need to remember the actual address at all. They therefore have no excuse not to write! The use of address books is described in the chapter *Managing your e-mail*, starting on page 61.

When giving out your e-mail address by other means, always be careful to place dots accurately and to spell each word correctly, otherwise messages will not reach you. Some e-mail addresses are case-sensitive, that is, if the address registered with the service provider contains capital letters, you must use them or the mail may not get through. Your service provider should inform you if this is the case. Unfortunately, an e-mail server cannot guess that fred@brit-computers.co is actually fred@british-computers.co.uk: instead the message will just be returned to the person who sent it, with a message indicating that the recipient was unknown.

If you want anyone outside your circle of known friends and family to be able to contact you, you can add yourself to one or more online directories, such as those described above. You should not be charged for an entry in any online directory. Be aware, however, that providing such information to the general public could result in your receiving junk e-mail, or *spam*, some of which may be of an extremely distasteful nature. See the section *Blocking messages* on page 66 for details of how to prevent this.

If you change your e-mail address, don't forget to tell people. Some suggestions for the best way to manage an address change are given on page 119.

Security considerations

Security is a big issue for all Internet traffic, both e-mail and other transactions. Electronic communication is prey to *hackers*, who can tap into the information and read its content while it is en route or stored on a server. Then there are the authorities that want to be able to read your mail to make sure you're behaving yourself ...

Hackers and the non-privacy of mail

You may wonder why anyone would bother reading your personal messages. The answer is that, as with other forms of mail interception, they are probably not specifically looking for a chatty letter to your brother, but for something more useful, and open everything in the hope of finding it. If you were sending a message to a company requesting goods, for example, they would immediately have your name and address, e-mail address, and possibly banking or credit card details or delivery information if you have provided them. For corporate e-mail, industrial espionage is big business, and hackers have been known to operate on behalf of one company, political party or pressure group against another to procure sensitive information for their employer.

To call any e-mail exchange 'private' is a misnomer, although this term is frequently used online; you can almost guarantee that if you send something confidential, risqué, potentially offensive or newsworthy to another person via e-mail, someone else will read it, and not only hackers – either the original recipient will forward it to someone else (and they to someone else, and so on, ad infinitum) or it will be read by a system administrator or over the recipient's shoulder by a colleague. Remember also that most systems automatically scan e-mail for certain key words or word combinations, such as abusive retorts or obscenities, and messages containing these items are automatically rejected.

Someone's watching you ...

The openness of the Internet and world-wide accessibility to e-mail is essential for its purpose, but it can also be open to abuse for criminal purposes. This is one reason why the governments of many countries are trying to implement

Internet and e-mail surveillance: the Internet is taking over from the mobile phone as the communication method preferred by the criminal. The proposals vary from one country to another, but in most cases include the right to examine, without your knowledge, the content of any file or e-mail message sent or received by you, or any record of your Internet use held on your or your service provider's computers. If you *encrypt* your mail, you may be required to submit all encryption passwords to your service provider or the government under such legislation, to ensure the encrypted messages contain no criminal material. Already service providers are being asked to hand over the passwords held on their own computers.

Each time such surveillance is proposed there is an outcry from those in favour of the freedom of information currently offered by the Internet, but the authorities counter that no one wants criminals to prosper, particularly at the expense of other Internet users (although the level of crime they aim to prevent is as yet undetermined). Whether the non-criminal majority wishes to have its own or a foreign government scrutinising personal or business e-mail is less publicly discussed; and to what degree such surveillance will prevail is as yet unclear, although it seems that one key measure will be to force all service providers to reveal details of their subscribers to the governments in their country of operation. Many of those in the business of providing Internet services believe this will simply drive the criminal element to use service providers based in other, non-regulated countries, leaving the government to invade only the privacy of the innocent. Despite pressure on the government by service providers and other businesses, it is almost inevitable that some level of world-wide government surveillance will come into place if the Internet continues to expand at its present rate, especially with media reports suggesting an increase in the incidence and variety of crime on the Internet.

Whatever our reservations over a government effectively tapping our personal e-mail, most of us would welcome action taken on those who pollute the Internet with obscene, racist or inflammatory material or who use it to carry out criminal activities such as credit card fraud. So if the proposed surveillance helps to combat this, it is not all bad news.

What security do I need?

Even if you can't prevent the government and its agents from reading your mail, it is worth preventing any other unauthorised person from doing so. The level of security you need depends on:

- What you intend to use e-mail for.

- Where or to whom you will be sending messages.

- What security is used or available to your recipients.

If you have a home or shared computer, and intend to send only messages and photographs to your family and friends, you probably need minimal security – unless you are a 'celebrity' or your photos are risqué or commercially valuable. You should be aware though that anyone can tap into your communication and copy it, including any photographs: it is not unknown for people to find their snaps on another website, perhaps having been tinkered with along the way. Usually such adaptations are intended to be funny rather than malicious, but it is still an invasion of privacy and in some cases can have distasteful intent. Be particularly wary of sending photographs of anyone – especially children – less than fully clothed, such as on the beach or in the bath. Compress or encode photographs when sending to help reduce the chance of interception. Remember that if you have connection to the Internet, nothing on your PC is secure or inaccessible to a hacker, and to be doubly safe from intrusion, always disconnect from the Internet and switch off the power when you finish using your computer, even if you do not have to pay for Internet usage.

If you are using e-mail only within an organisation in which no one is able to send e-mail to external addresses, you can probably do without advanced security unless the data is of a particularly confidential nature. Your intranet will have an inbuilt level of security, including a firewall. This is a series of programs, often running on a separate server outside the main intranet, that monitor incoming and outgoing items, for example to prevent access by hackers; reject undesirable information sent by e-mail, such as viruses or pornography; and to prevent anything secure or confidential from leaving the company without authorisation. You may be asked to encode certain information, particularly confidential or commercially-sensitive documents, if you are required to send it by e-mail to a contact outside the intranet, to make doubly sure it will not be intercepted.

If you will be sending specifications for products, quotes for work, or similar items via e-mail to customers or suppliers, you must think about security. If all the information is provided in attached documents, you might be able to password the documents rather than implementing direct security on your e-mail, but you will need to make the recipient aware of the password by a method other than e-mail, otherwise a hacker could capture both. If you require further security, you might wish to encrypt or encode your e-mail. Encryption is available in many forms, one of which is the *digital certificate* (sometimes called a digital signature or digital ID). Not all e-mail software supports this function, but it is becoming more widely used by business for legal, confidential or sensitive documents, and will probably become the norm for business e-mail sent via the Internet. Some additional information on encryption and digital certificates is provided in *E-mail allsorts,* starting on page 105; as the functions available vary from one e-mail application to another, check your own software's manuals and online help for specific details of how to implement security for your product. If you are working within a company, ask the people responsible for running your intranet if you need more information on the security options available to you.

The further your e-mail is going, and the more servers or *gateways* it has to pass through, the higher the possibility of it being tampered with. For example, there are far more oppor-tunities for hackers to operate on a message going from an individual in France to a company in Pakistan than on a message going from one person within a small company to another e-mail user in the same company. Each time your message goes from a secure server on to the general telephone network, it is exposed to the possibility of interference from hackers.

There is no point having tamper-proof security measures in place if the recipients of your messages do not operate a similar level of security. If they send replies to your messages in unencrypted, standard format, with the original message quoted, the same hackers who were unable to access your encrypted or digitally signed mail might get the chance they need. If your data is sensitive, always insist that recipients answer your e-mail in the same encrypted format in which it was sent.

Avoiding computer viruses

A computer *virus* is a program or instruction that causes damage to the software on a computer. It is called a virus because it exhibits behaviour similar to a biological virus, in that it is infectious, making it easy to 'catch' and even easier to spread. Viruses are usually small, hidden programs, the presence of which you are unaware until they start to operate. They cause damage either by deleting or corrupting data, or by issuing commands that cause the computer to stop completely. Sometimes it is possible to resolve virus problems through the use of software 'antidotes', but often by this time the damage has already been done and might not be fully reversible.

Before e-mail and the Internet were in common use, viruses were propagated mainly via floppy disks: when a user inserted a disk containing a virus, a copy was transferred to the hard drive, and then copied to each successive floppy disk inserted into the machine. It is easy to see how quickly such a virus could spread, especially in a work environment where many people might use a common set of disks to install software.

Unfortunately, e-mail has only made the problem more prevalent. Now viruses on your hard disk can send themselves outside your organisation by attaching themselves to e-mail messages and attachments. The creators of viruses can send them to Internet sites and users as e-mail attachments, or hidden in seemly innocent files that you might download from a website or *FTP* site.

If a file sent as an attachment contains a virus, it could potentially damage not only the recipient's computer but also any other users to whom the message is forwarded. Some particularly advanced viruses, called *worms*, will seek out information on your system regarding other e-mail users – such as entries in your address book, or even folders containing your received e-mail messages – and automatically forward themselves to those users, before destroying your own system. This sets up a chain reaction that can spread extremely quickly and has a devastating effect, particularly on in-house intranet systems where it is common for all users to be listed in each user's address book. One such worm, called the Love Bug, or ILOVEYOU, was created and distributed by a single programmer early in May 2000. Within two days it had spread to systems all over the world and caused damage estimated at $11 billion, primarily to intranets in large companies, despite an antidote being made available within that time. Many companies lost valuable data and were unable to operate at full capacity for some considerable time.

The best protection against viruses is to obtain, install and use reputable virus detection (anti-virus) software. Use it daily – more frequently if you receive many messages per day – and update it regularly. This is essential to protect the data on your computer from potential virus damage: if the software captures only one virus sent to you via e-mail or on a disk it will have paid for itself many times over. Be aware, however, that no virus detection software will guarantee protection against every virus. For protection to be available, a virus must be known about and an antidote be made available and downloaded to your computer. Antidotes are usually available fairly quickly, but it is up to you to download them in order to protect your system, and they might not rectify damage already caused by a virus, so it is still important to back up your system regularly.

The golden rule on preventing virus attack via e-mail is never to open any message attachment from someone you don't know, even if you do have virus protection. For further advice on this topic, see *Attachments and computer viruses* on page 89. Some addresses for websites offering virus detection software are given in the appendix *Useful Internet addresses*.

Legal issues

The legal consequences of sending an e-mail message are not always obvious. In many parts of the world, the information given in an e-mail has little legal standing under contract law, so if you accepted an order by e-mail from one of these countries, the contract to purchase might not be legally binding on both parties. This will probably change as e-mail becomes more widely used for business communication and more sophisticated, but meanwhile care must be taken with international negotiations by e-mail.

One major legal problem with e-mail is that it cannot be signed, and therefore it cannot be proved who actually sent a particular message, but with the use of digital certificates and signatures increasing, this might change: in some countries a digital certificate is already legally recognised as the equivalent of a standard signature. Until this applies everywhere, however, e-mail is not the answer for all communications, particularly international contracts, and in many cases you will need to revert to traditional mail or other methods – for time-sensitive or confidential information in particular.

In many other areas of the legal system, e-mail is treated the same as any other form of communication. For example, the writer of a libellous e-mail message could be taken to court in most countries. In many places e-mail can now be used as supporting evidence in court cases, and although this is limited in its extent you should treat all messages as potentially usable in a court of law.

You can find more detailed information on the legal status of e-mail in the section *Legal considerations* on page 117.

Observing netiquette

Although e-mail is supposed to be fairly informal, the medium has built up a form of etiquette or code of conduct to ensure that the writers of e-mail do not irritate or offend their readers. This is often referred to as 'netiquette', and is particularly applicable when sending e-mail messages to a newsgroup or list (see the chapter *Communicating with others* on page 96). The most important points of netiquette for everyday e-mail are described below. Further details can be found on the Internet by searching for the word 'netiquette'.

If you are accused of breaking netiquette, it is best to apologise as soon as possible, and if you are not sure what you have done wrong, ask.

Shouting

Using block capital letters is considered to be the equivalent of shouting and should be avoided. It's acceptable to use block capitals if you are sending a short e-mail to proclaim an achievement and express excitement, for example 'WE'VE GOT THE CONTRACT!', but in general, capital letters are difficult to read en bloc and thus cause irritation to the reader. Many recipients will simply delete a message written solely in capitals, so it is best to avoid them wherever possible. Be sensible: would you read a book or a newspaper article written entirely in capitals? You'd be hard pressed to find one.

This applies only to block capitals – you should still use single capitals where needed at the start of sentences and proper nouns. Some people use no capitals in e-mail at all, but this can be confusing and almost as difficult to read as block capitals.

Flaming

Flaming is the electronic equivalent of losing your temper or being overly aggressive, and usually results from someone reading a controversial comment and sending a hasty and ill-considered reply. Always read through your message before you send, and remove any angry or rude comments. If you wish to make a comment that you think might provoke an angry response, try to take the sting out of it by preceding it with a statement like this:

//Flameproof suit on...//

as this shows you realise the nature of the statement and are open to reasoned argument. This is not carte blanche to be rude, insulting or abusive, and should only ever be used in personal messages or in postings to newsgroups/lists where such an approach – and the provocative comment it precedes – would be appreciated for what it is.

Humour

Don't try to be funny or sarcastic. E-mail does not translate humour very well because the person cannot see your face. Sarcasm in particular can come across as sincere. Remember: once a message has been sent, you cannot retrieve it. It is possible to use humour in personal e-mail to friends, especially if you indicate it with an appropriate emoticon, but only if they will understand it (see *Abbreviations and codes* on page 121).

State your subject

Always give the message a title by filling in the Subject line. It helps to tell the recipient what your e-mail is about before they open it, and it also helps you to file it correctly. If you are responding to a message, use the Reply function to copy the subject from that message automatically, and precede it with 'Re:'.

Make sure the subject of the message reflects its content. This is particularly important for users of newsgroups and forums who might be involved in exchanges of e-mail on various topics. It is very annoying to those who sort their mail by *thread* to find an unrelated item in an existing thread. (A thread is a message topic: see *Setting display options* on page 72 for details.) For example, if you were following a discussion on a cookery newsgroup about the best way to make a raspberry soufflé, you would not expect to find a query on how to boil potatoes. This error normally results from someone using the reply function to write an unrelated message to the same list, rather than starting a new message.

Remember, unless you are replying to a specific message on a specific topic, start a new message instead. Even if there is an element of commonality, it is best to start afresh: if you want to write about raspberry jam or cheese soufflé, start a new message. This also works in reverse: don't start another thread about raspberry soufflé, use the reply function to add your thoughts on the topic so that anyone interested in raspberry soufflé has all the information in one place.

In unsolicited mail, always use a question mark (?) as the first character in the subject line. For example, if you are trying to locate someone via a shared address or an address you have found in a directory, use a subject like this:

?Are you James Mason previously of Yorktown, WI?

Check the address

Always check an e-mail address is correct before sending your message. It is all too easy to mistype an address: many addresses are very similar, especially those used by companies, and it is not possible to cancel an e-mail once sent. Don't assume, for example, that John Brown who works at StarTools plc has an e-mail address of john_brown@startools.com – there may be another John Brown there and it could be someone in a senior position who will not welcome your intrusion into his mailbox, particularly if your message is of a personal nature. Such an error could backfire on you and your intended recipient.

If you are not 100 per cent certain of an address, check with your intended recipient first. This is particularly the case if you have located an address via a directory listing on the Internet; you may think you know the only Sandra Chase in Cape Town, but you could be wrong. If writing on spec to see whether you have the right person, be polite. Ask a pertinent question in the subject line, prefixing it with a question mark as described above (for example, ?Are you the Sandra Chase who previously worked at EdCo?), offer an apology in case you have contacted the wrong person, and leave it at that. If you have managed to find the right person, he or she will probably contact you. Under no circumstances should you follow such an approach with another message if you have had no response: it could be that you have located the wrong person or that the person does not wish to communicate with you further.

Most e-mail software these days allows you to save e-mail addresses in an address book. This is recommended for people with whom you regularly correspond as it saves a lot of typing and the potential for mistyping. Details of how to use an address book are given in the chapter *Managing your e-mail*, starting on page 61.

Security
Don't send anything confidential by e-mail. Remember that e-mail can be easily read by other people. Anything private should be sent in a conventional sealed letter, not over the Internet. See *Security considerations* on page 43 for more security-related information.

Hiring and firing
Don't use e-mail to hire or fire people; it is very bad manners and in some countries e-mail is not a legally recognisable form of correspondence on such issues. While there are now many Internet portal sites that advertise jobs and allow you to tender for work via e-mail across the Internet, these should only ever be used for initial contact to exchange names, addresses and informal bids. Any advance should always be followed up with a conventional letter.

Rules for replies

When replying to someone, you can quote parts of his or her original message. Insert a chevron (>) before a line containing a quotation. Most e-mail software allows you to do this quite easily by selecting the Reply function; it then automatically copies the original e-mail and places > in front of each line. You may then delete lines as you wish: insert <snip> to indicate where you have cut out information. Never take quotes out of context in order to change their meaning, and always acknowledge the origin of the text. This is particularly important when writing to newsgroups or lists where recipients of your message might not have read the original from which you are quoting.

Style

We will look at style in more detail in the next section, but netiquette plays a part here too. Many e-mail applications now offer a variety of 'stationery' on which to type your e-mail. This is fine for personal messages, but do not use it for business, unless instructed to do so by someone of appropriate seniority, or for postings to lists and newsgroups. For these purposes, write plain text on a plain background. Within a company, you might be able to use *HTML* to improve the appearance of your messages (you can find more about HTML on page 105), but do not use it for external messages, or for postings to lists and groups, as not every e-mail user is able to read HTML: it depends on which software they are using.

If you are sending attachments such as images, sound or video clips, it is good practice to establish beforehand whether your recipient knows how to deal with them. Make sure they have the correct level of software and if not, where they can find it. Software to display or play common file formats is often available free on the manufacturer's website. If not, there is usually a trial version available for download that allows a recipient simply to view or listen to the attachment without providing the full functions of the product.

Guidelines on layout and style

E-mail is generally recognised as a less formal form of communication than the letter, and there are few rules about layout. Postal addresses are rarely shown; dates are automatically generated; often there is not even a salutation or closing line. The appearance can be very plain, if written in plain text as is the norm, or more jazzy if HTML is used. Messages can be personalised to your own tastes and to show your personal details if required.

Plain text or HTML?

HTML, or Hypertext Mark-up Language, is the computer language of the Internet. Like most word-processing formats, it is basically a coding system for text that tells the computer how to display it in terms of colour, typeface, emphasis, alignment and size. In general the coding is hidden from view and you see only the formatted text, but if you do not have the facility to view HTML, it will appear as plain text.

Generally, if a document is long enough to warrant a lot of emphasis, highlighting or differentiation in the text, it should be created with a word processor and sent as an e-mail attachment, rather than as a simple message.

Further information on using HTML is provided in the chapter *E-mail allsorts*, starting on page 105.

Wrapping lines in a message

No matter how neatly you style and lay out your message, it might not appear the same on the recipient's screen, even if you write it in plain text. One reason for this is the word wrap function, which sets the length of text lines in a message. Most users set this to 80 characters or less to eliminate either the need to scroll right and left to read all the text, in e-mail products that do not automatically wrap lines, or messy line breaks in applications that do wrap lines. If the recipient's word wrap setting is different from your own, the message can look totally different on their screen, with lines breaking halfway through. For example, in the messages below, the first has word wrap set at 85 characters, the second at 45. You can see how the lines are automatically wrapped in the upper example, whereas in the lower they are somewhat ragged.

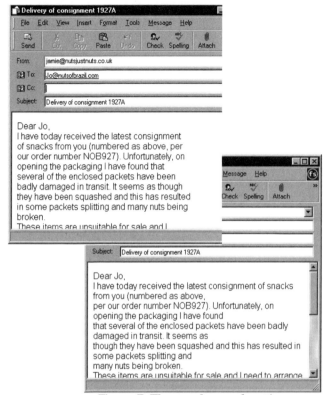

Figure 7: The word wrap function

There are a couple of points to note when setting word wrap:

- Many newsgroup servers will not display more than 80 characters per line.

- When text from a message is quoted in a reply, it is usually prefaced with an extra character (usually a chevron: >). If your message might be quoted, set word wrap to 70 characters per line or less to prevent the need to scroll across the page.

In Microsoft® Outlook Express, you set word wrap by selecting **Options** from the **Tools** menu, then selecting the **Send** page tab, and clicking on the **Plain Text Settings** button. This displays a window in which you can specify the exact number of characters per line. By default it is set to 76 characters per line.

There are some utilities offered on the Internet for tidying up and formatting e-mail and resolving such issues as inconsistent word wrapping. For example, the website for Roundhill Software (www.roundhillsoftware.com) offers a product called Message Cleaner.

Signing your messages

While you cannot physically sign an e-mail with a pen, most people have an *electronic signature* that they apply to each message. (This is not the same as a digital signature, which is another name for the digital certificate security feature.) If using HTML, a graphic of the person's actual signature can be included, but more commonly an electronic signature shows just a name and contact information. This can comprise a number of lines. Some people include a drawing made from keyboard characters, a motto or a favourite quote, to make their messages more personal. An example is shown after the sender's name in Figure 8.

Most e-mail applications allow you to generate and save such a signature as a separate file, and then either append it automatically to each e-mail message or add it when required. If you are working in a large organisation, you may be issued with guidelines on how your electronic signature should look and when to use it. Otherwise use your own discretion. Many large companies have a standard signature applied to all e-mail

```
Mr Jones,

Thank you for your order for 10kg of organic cherry
tomatoes. Unfortunately we have sold our entire
crop, but another organic farm has agreed to fulfil
your order on our behalf and the tomatoes will be
delivered to you by 0800 tomorrow morning.

If you require any other produce, please contact us.
Thank you,

Fred Smith
    (*)                                          (*)
    (*)*) "Fresh fruit, fresher by design" (*(*)
    \^^^/                                    \^^^/
The Organic Fruit Co, Little Farm, Grupton, ST4 7HW
Call: (+726) 123 124323 or fax: (+726) 8263514
Email: fredthefarmer@organicfruits.co.uk
```

Figure 8: An example of an e-mail 'signature'

leaving the company, which contains security and disclaimer information and which often appears at the top, rather than the bottom, of each message.

It is possible to have more than one signature, so you might want to generate several variations, each to be used for a different type of e-mail (for example, one for personal messages to friends, another for business messages, and another for newsgroup postings).

In Microsoft® Outlook Express, you create a signature by selecting **Options** from the **Tools** menu, and selecting the **Signatures** page of the notebook.

Adding pictures

You can attach graphics to an e-mail message, of course, but it will depend on the recipient's set-up whether or not those images are visible in the position you place them, that is, *inline*, or are merely attached to the end of the document. Inline images are shown as such only if the recipient's software can handle HTML. Placing large images inline is not recommended as it takes a long time to send (upload) and receive (download) large files.

Sending attachments

If you are sending a large file, whether text or graphics, you should compress it first using a *zip* or *compression program*. Such programs are often pre-installed as part of your computer's operating system. If not you can download shareware or freeware versions from the Internet. When you send a compressed file as an attachment to an e-mail message, it helps the recipient if you specify which compression program you used. The recipient has to decompress the file at the other end before viewing it. Generally, zip programs are not readable across different operating systems; that is, if you zip a file on a PC running Windows®, a Mac, AIX or Linux user might be unable to unzip it, even if you provide the unzip program.

Sources for some of the most popular compression programs are given in the appendix *Useful Internet addresses*.

In the next chapter we look at ways to manage your e-mail. It is best to consider this before you even start to send and receive mail, as this helps you to be more organised and methodical in your correspondence.

CHAPTER 4

Managing your e-mail

By default, all e-mail sent to you will be received into a single mailbox, and copies of all messages you send will be stored in a single folder. If you will use e-mail only for infrequent or personal messages, this might be sufficient. If you will be sending messages to the same people frequently or to many different people in different organisations, or if more than one person will use your e-mail software, consider managing your mail in a more structured way or you will never be able to find anything. Set this up before you start sending or receiving messages, to minimise disruption.

In this chapter we look at the various ways in which you can organise and manage your e-mail. This includes setting up folders for your mail, like a filing cabinet; setting up address books and distribution lists, to save a lot of typing; directing mail automatically according to its content; and filtering mail to remove 'junk' items. To make it easier to understand how some of these functions are used, we follow a fictional character, Peter Jones, as he sets up options to improve his e-mail management.

Setting up a filing system

Few people enjoy filing. With paper correspondence you have no choice, but with electronic mail it is usually optional. If you don't have a lot of messages and only use e-mail to correspond with friends and family, you might prefer to leave all your received messages in the inbox, and the sent messages in the sent folder. However, if you are running a business, or use your e-mail account for both business and personal use, it is worth setting up *folders* (sometimes called mailboxes) for your mail, to make it easier to locate items when you need them.

Setting up a filing system using folders is easy. Let's look at an example, using Microsoft® Outlook Express. We will follow this example through most of the tasks described here.

Peter Jones is the Marketing Manager of ZedCo Limited. He is responsible for dealing with the company's public relations agency, PRCo; its Sales Division, managed by Carol Herbert; and the managers of various projects. Each sends him e-mail on a regular basis, to which he often needs to reply.

Peter's inbox is becoming crammed and disorganised, so he wants to set up some folders. He needs to create separate folders for each of his main contacts, so he can keep all his messages from each in the same place. So he selects **New** from the **File** menu, and selects the **Folder** option. This displays the Create Folder window, shown in Figure 9.

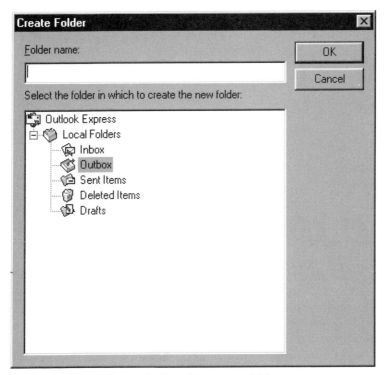

Figure 9: Creating a new folder

Peter types the name of his first new folder, PRCo, and selects the Local Folders item in the existing folders list to create the PRCo folder at the same level as his inbox. He selects **OK**, and the new folder appears in the folder list. He can now repeat this sequence for each new folder. He can even add different levels of folder; for example, Peter could create a Projects folder containing separate subfolders for each project. The resulting folder list looks like this:

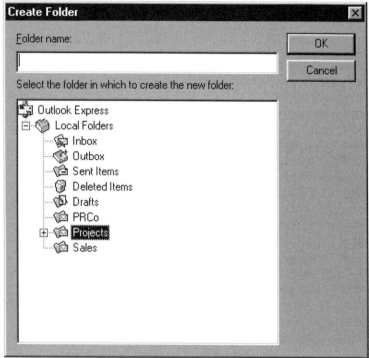

Figure 10: A list of created folders

Note the plus sign next to the Projects folder. This indicates that Peter has set up folders within Projects, as described above. To view the folders, Peter just clicks on the plus sign.

Peter can now transfer messages to the relevant folders whenever he wants. To do this, he selects each message and drags it (by holding down the mouse button while moving the mouse) to the name of the folder he wants to place the message in, then releases the mouse button to move the message.

While this is quite sufficient for most users, there is an easier way with some applications, which automates the whole filing process. This is part of the message filtering function, and thus is described in the section *Filtering e-mail*, starting on page 66.

Setting up address books

Most e-mail applications these days allow you to store details of your regular correspondents in an address book (sometimes called 'Contacts'). This is useful as it saves a lot of retyping and minimises the chance of mistyping an address. Some software adds details to the address book automatically for each person to whom you send mail. This is not always wise, especially if you send mail to many people only once, as the details will require a lot of disk storage, but you can usually turn off such features, if you prefer.

Once an address is in your address book, you can simply select it from a list to send a message to that person, or start typing the address or the nickname you have assigned to that person in a message and the software will complete it for you.

Using Peter Jones from our previous example, let's look at how to set up an entry in an address book.

Peter often sends e-mail messages to Carol Herbert. Although he is usually replying to a message she has sent, and therefore does not need to type the address, he does sometimes need to send a message that is not a reply, or forward a message from someone else, so he needs to provide Carol's e-mail address in the **To:** line. Peter cannot always remember the address and has to look it up. He decides to create an address book entry instead, so he can automatically select Carol's name and no longer need to know the exact placing of dots and symbols.

Remember, Peter uses Microsoft® Outlook Express. To create an address book entry, he selects the **Addresses** button from the toolbar, or **Address Book** from the **Tools** menu. This displays the address book shown in Figure 11 on page 62. Peter's address book already has some entries – yours might be blank.

From here, Peter selects the **New Message** button from the toolbar, and selects **New Contact** from the drop-down menu. (The other options on this menu are usually used to create lists of people to send to – we will look at this in the next section.) The notebook shown in Figure 12 overleaf appears.

In Microsoft® Outlook Express, there are a number of pages of information for each contact, so you can include all sorts of detail in an address book entry (although this is not so with all e-mail software – in some you can only enter e-mail address and

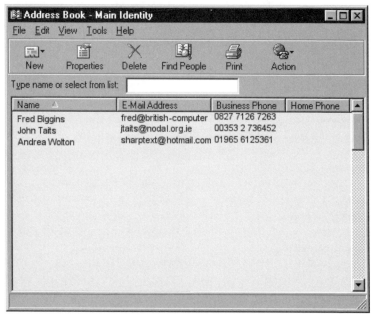

Figure 11: The address book

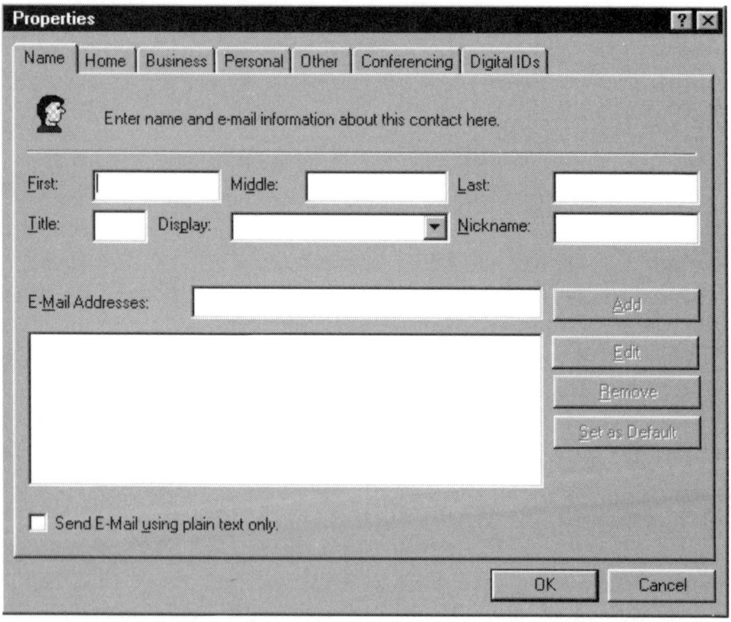

Figure 12: Adding a new contact to the address book

telephone number). It's a very useful way of keeping information about your contacts in one place, so that whether you need to phone, e-mail, fax or write a letter to them, you know where to find all the relevant information. You can even include personal details such as birthdays. However, there is no obligation to enter all this information – most people just use the address book for entering e-mail addresses to save the need to retype. Indeed, there is an argument for not including too much information, in case the computer is stolen, for example. You might also need to be careful about the level of information you include about a customer on your computer, so as not to contravene legislation relating to data protection. This varies from one country to another, so it is advisable to check first before storing information on a large number of contacts. It is unlikely to be a problem if you are only entering details of friends and relations.

Now back to Peter. He wants to include Carol Herbert as a contact, so he types information into the contact notebook, as shown in Figure 13. He uses 'carol' as the nickname, and also includes Carol's private e-mail address in case he needs to send

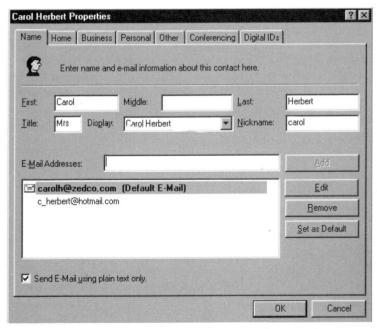

Figure 13: Contact details for the address book

her a message when she is not at work. When he has finished entering the information, he selects **OK** to save this as a new entry, and Carol's name now appears in the list in the main Address Book window.

You can print the contents of your address book in most e-mail applications. This is useful if you are going to be away from your computer and need the contact information. You can print details of all the entries, or select specific entries to print. To do this in Microsoft® Outlook Express, open the Address Book window (shown in Figure 11), select names if required, and click the **Print** button on the toolbar. You are offered the choice of three layouts:

Selecting:	Prints
Memo	All address book information for each contact
Business card	Company name, business phone number, e-mail address
Phone list	Telephone numbers only.

We will look at selecting names from an address book in the chapter *Sending e-mail*, starting on page 77.

Setting up distribution lists

So now we know how to add an individual's details to an address book. What if you want to send messages to a group of people? Well, you could type all the e-mail address details for each individually, or add each person to your address book and select them individually, each time you want to send a message, but this is rather time-consuming. Why not create a list of all these people, and simply select the list name each time you want to send a message to them all?

In Microsoft® Outlook Express, this function is known as 'groups'. In other e-mail products, the terms 'list' or 'distribution list' are used.

Let's go back to Peter Jones. As previously mentioned, he receives mail from a number of managers of different projects, and sends mail to them as well. There are a number of issues common to all projects, on which he needs to communicate with all the managers. He does this by sending a single message to them all.

Peter has already discovered the usefulness of the address book, as shown in the previous section. Since adding Carol's name, he has included details of all his business contacts. So now, all he needs to do to save even more typing is add a list entry, comprising the names of all the managers in his group.

To do this, Peter selects the **Addresses** button on the toolbar, or **Address Book** from the **Tools** menu to display the address book (shown previously in Figure 11 on page 62). From this window, Peter selects the **New** button on the toolbar, and **New Group** from the drop-down menu. This displays the window shown in Figure 14.

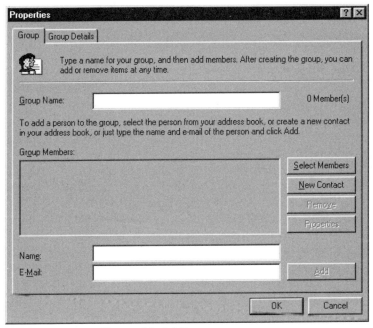

Figure 14: Adding a new group

First Peter types a name for the group, in this case Project Managers. As Peter already has the names of the individuals defined in his address book, he simply selects **Select Members** to display the address book, and clicks on each of the names in turn from the contacts list to add them to the group. If he finds there is one he has forgotten, he can either add the details by typing them in the **Name** and **E-mail** fields at the bottom of the window, or can add the name as a new contact to the address book by selecting **New Contact**. If he selects someone by mistake, he can select **Remove** to remove that name from the list. If selected from the address book, the person's details are retained in the address book for future use, and just deleted from this particular group.

When Peter has finished identifying group members, he selects **OK** to save the group details and return to the address book. The new group, Project Managers, is added to the list of contacts in the Address Book window, but shows a different icon to identify it as a group.

When Peter wants to send mail to this group, he can now type or select the group name as the addressee (see the chapter *Sending e-mail* on page 77 for details) and the message will be sent to all the members of the group automatically.

Filtering e-mail

Some e-mail software is quite sophisticated in what it can automate for you. Most of the mainstream products now offer some form of filtering, allowing you to automatically redirect incoming mail to other users or to specific folders, or to block mail from certain senders. (Unfortunately this does not apply to many of the free e-mail sites, which offer a reduced set of functions. However, some such sites do now offer basic filtering and filing methods, so it is worth checking.) Filtering may also be applied at a different level by businesses, for example to prevent you from sending mail outside the organisation, but this is applied by the server, so is not described here.

Filtering can be a very useful function. If, for example, you are regularly receiving junk mail or mail from Internet sites you have visited which you do not know how to stop, you can enter the sender's e-mail address and any further messages from that sender will be redirected away from your mailbox. Filtering can also provide a useful, time-saving method of automatic filing. Let's look at each of these in turn.

Blocking messages

Poor old Peter Jones. He is being harassed by e-mail by a company trying to sell him computer parts. When browsing the Internet, looking for information on the latest modems, Peter inadvertently left his e-mail address with the site, and has been added to an automatic mailing list. So every time the supplier issues a message via their mailing list, Peter receives a copy. He has tried replying to these messages, asking to be removed from the list, but to no avail. Although he deletes the messages as soon as they arrive, they are still causing a nuisance.

There is a solution, and it is incredibly easy to use. Peter can add the details of the sender to his Blocked Senders list, and will never again see a mail message sent from that address.

There are two ways to do this. Which you choose depends on whether you have a message from that sender already in your mailbox.

As Peter has just received a message from the supplier, he can use this to his advantage. He selects the unwelcome message from the inbox, and selects **Block Sender** from the **Message** menu. A message pops up to inform Peter that this e-mail address has been added to his Blocked Senders list. That's it – an easy solution to an annoying problem.

Even if Peter had already removed all the mail, if he knew the sending address he could still block the sender, by selecting **Message Rules** from the **Tools** menu, and **Blocked Senders** from the drop-down list. This displays the Blocked Senders page of the Rules notebook, as shown in Figure 15.

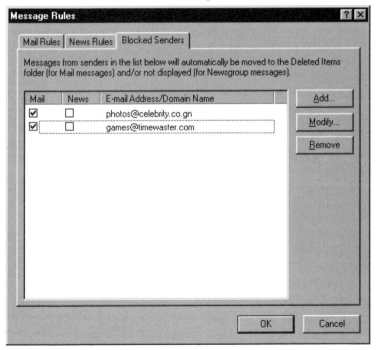

Figure 15: Blocking unwanted e-mail

Although this is the first time Peter has blocked a sender, there are some entries already in his list. If you use e-mail at work, you might find that some entries are pre-set like this, often to prevent you from receiving mail from outside agencies.

To block the sender, Peter selects **Add**. This displays the window shown in Figure 16.

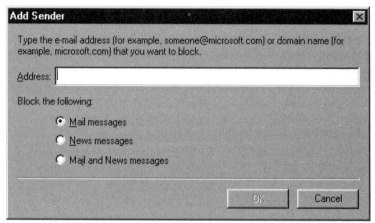

Figure 16: Adding a new blocked sender to the list

Peter types the e-mail address from which the offending messages are being sent, and selects **OK**. In this case, he is blocking e-mail messages only, which is the default action, so he needs not select an option from the list; if he was receiving mail from newsgroups (see the chapter *Communicating with others*) and wished to block messages emanating from this sender via these groups as well, he could select one of the other two options as appropriate before selecting **OK**.

If Peter later found that he was missing the messages, and in fact did want to know about discounted computer parts, he can simply remove the blocking by returning to this window, selecting the relevant entry in the list, and selecting **Remove**, and the mail will start arriving again when the supplier next sends a message.

One important thing to note about blocking: it relies on a single address being used to send the junk mail. Many junk mailers propagate numerous e-mail addresses from which to bombard you with information, so you might still receive some messages from the most persistent of offenders. Some products, such as MSN™ Hotmail®, now offer inbox protection that works in reverse: it allows you to specify those people from whom you *do* want to receive mail, and all other incoming mail is placed in a single folder, kept for up to 30 days and then deleted. This is a good way to sort the important from the trivial, but remember to scan the non-specified mail regularly or you may miss messages that could be of interest, such as those from a contact with a new e-mail address, or a query from a old friend or potential client.

Automating your filing with rules and filters

With most e-mail applications that support filtering, there is no need to spend hours filing individual messages and attachments – you can get your e-mail software to do it for you! Such applications allow you to automate message filing by specifying rules to determine the destination of incoming messages. Such rules can be based on one or more of the following criteria:

- Who sent the message (name, nickname or ID).

- Who the message is addressed to (name, nickname or ID).

- Text appearing in the subject line, or the body of the message.

- The security or priority level assigned to the message.

- Whether the message contains attachments.

Some applications also apply such rules automatically to outgoing mail, but this is less common. You can, however, manually apply existing rules to your sent mail to file these items in the same way as incoming mail.

Let's look at our example using Microsoft® Outlook Express.

Currently Peter's mail arrives in his inbox, and he manually transfers the messages to the folders once he has read them. As he is receiving more and more messages each day, Peter is getting tired of spending so much time filing his messages by hand. So let's look at how Peter could set up mail rules to direct his incoming mail into the relevant folders automatically, rather than into his inbox, starting with messages from PRCo.

Messages from PRCo could come from a number of different e-mail users within the company. However, all e-mail sent from PRCo includes the name of the company in the message signature (see pages 55–56), so a rule can be set up based on this.

To create a new rule, Peter selects **Message Rules** from the **Tools** menu, and selects the **Mail Rules** option. (Note that other e-mail applications may use different names for this feature, for example, in QUALCOMM® Eudora®, this option is called **Filters**.) This displays the window shown in Figure 17. (However, if you have no rules set up you might find that the window shown in Figure 18 appears instead, in which case simply close this window and that shown in Figure 17 will be displayed.)

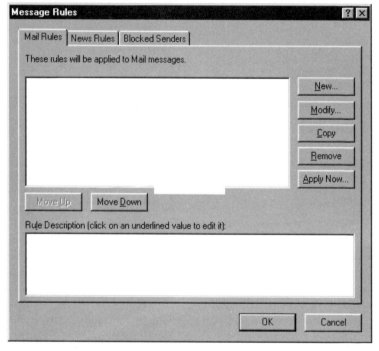

Figure 17: Defining rules for your mail

Peter selects **New** to create a rule. This displays another rules window, shown in Figure 18 opposite.

By clicking in the relevant boxes, Peter specifies the following conditions and actions:

"Where the message body contains specific words, or where the Subject line contains specific words, move the message to the specified folder."

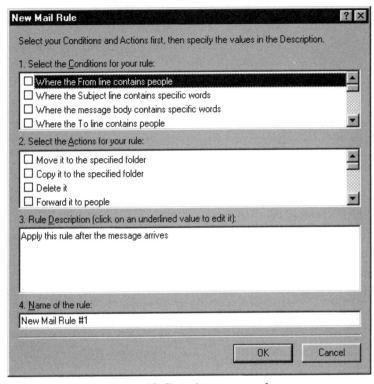

Figure 18: Creating a new rule

On selection the rules appear in the **Rule Description** box. Peter can now click on these rules in the box to edit the information to show the specific words to look for and the folder to move the messages to. Once this is complete, he edits the final box on this window to name his new rule, and clicks **OK**. The new rule is added to the rules list in the main **Message Rules** window, as shown in Figure 19 overleaf.

While working in this window, with the new rule shown, Peter can apply the rule to all his existing messages by selecting **Apply Now**. He is prompted to select a folder to which the rule will be applied (in this case, his over-crammed inbox), and on selecting **Apply Now** again, the existing messages are scanned, and any containing the word PRCo are automatically moved to the PRCo folder. Peter may repeat this exercise on his Sent Messages folder, to include all his responses to PRCo in the PRCo folder. He can also create automatic filing for his other

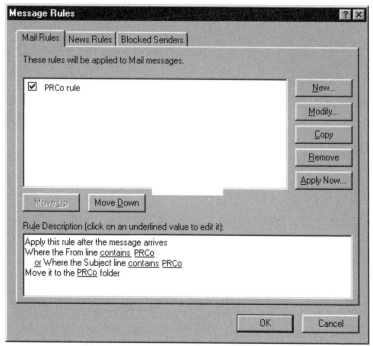

Figure 19: The new rule, ready for use

regular correspondents: for example, a rule to move anything containing the words 'Carol' or 'Sales' to a folder called 'Sales', and one or more for the projects with which he is involved.

Once Peter has created such rules for all his regular correspondents, he can sit back and wait for the mail to come in. As a mail message arrives, it will be scanned for compliance with any defined rules, and moved accordingly. Peter can still see when he has new messages, whatever folder they are in, because they will be highlighted as unread (usually shown in bold) as in Figure 20. He can then decide which ones to read first, without having to wade through a large, disorganised inbox.

Setting display options

When you first start using an e-mail product, you will probably be happy to stick with the layout with which it first appears; probably a multi-paned window comprising folder list, message list and a toolbar, with all messages appearing in date order.

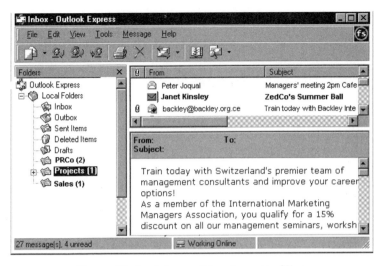

Figure 20: An inbox with automatic filing

Later you might find it useful to tailor the appearance of your e-mail to suit your own, specific needs. With most applications, you can select a number of display options to improve the appearance of your mail. Let's look at the most common ones, using Microsoft® Outlook Express as an example.

Showing and hiding messages

Most e-mail software allows you to control which messages you want to see. If you receive many messages in a day, you might prefer to show only those that you haven't previously read, hiding others from view without deleting them. (You can always change the setting back to view the hidden messages.) This is often a good idea if you receive many messages but need to retain them for future reference, rather than deleting each message after you have read and acted upon its content. However, it can also cause you to forget to delete messages you no longer require, making your e-mail software slow to start and prone to *crashes*.

Some products also allow you to set your own conditions for showing or hiding mail. This could include, for example, only showing messages that arrived in the past three days; only showing secure messages; or hiding messages with attachments.

To change the display of messages in Microsoft® Outlook Express, select **Current View** from the **View** menu, and select one of the options from the drop-down list.

Grouping messages by subject

This is unlikely to be appropriate unless you regularly receive mail from newsgroups or lists (see the chapter *Communicating with others* on page 96), or from one or more correspondents on the same topic, usually as a flow of message, reply, forward, further reply, and so on. In this case, all the messages will have the same subject line (prefixed with Re: or Fw: as appropriate).

By default, your messages will appear in your inbox in a 'flat' display, that is, one after the other in the order they were received by your server, regardless of subject. This is fine for most uses, but if you subscribe to newsgroups or much of your mail is question-and-answer based, you may prefer to switch to threaded display. This groups all related messages together in a hierarchy. An example of threaded display is shown in Figure 21.

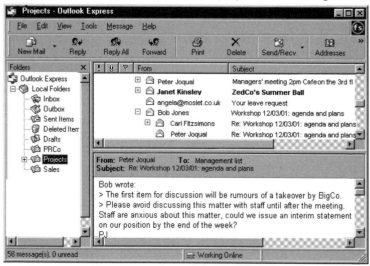

Figure 21: Using threaded display

Note the plus/minus sign to the left of some messages. These indicate a thread, or series of messages. The item next to this sign is usually the first in the sequence – most likely the original message to which the others are replies, forwards or comments. You can click on this plus/minus sign to expand or collapse the display of the thread. When plus shows, the thread is collapsed – only the top level message shows – when minus shows, the thread is expanded, with all messages showing. Sometimes you can have nested threads, as in the example above, so you might need to click on more than one plus to expand the whole thread fully.

To set your display to threaded in Microsoft® Outlook Express, select **Group Messages by Conversation** from the **View** menu.

Note that threaded displays only work if the person sends a reply or forward to the original e-mail message or newsgroup posting. Starting a new message using the same words in the subject line does not always have the same effect.

Sorting messages

Most e-mail software displays messages according to the date they were sent or received by the server. If you prefer, you can usually group messages by the person who sent them, the subject, the priority if one is specified, and so on. Which options are available to you will depend on which software you use, and what information has been specified for each message by the sender. There is no point, for example, in sorting your messages by priority if none of your correspondents ever specifies a priority for his or her messages. If you regularly receive mail from newsgroups or lists, it might be useful to group by subject, but it is often better to do this by threading (see above). If you receive mail from a few people only you might prefer to sort by sender, but remember that if you retain read messages you will need to scroll up and down through the inbox or folder to find the new messages if they are not sorted by date.

To change the sorting of messages in Microsoft® Outlook Express, select **Sort by** from the **View** menu, or simply click on one of the titles at the top of the inbox content list (for example, click on the title **From** to sort your mail by sender, or click on **Received** to sort it by date). You are usually offered two choices, ascending or descending order. For example, sorting by sender in ascending order sorts from A–Z, descending from Z–A.

Changing the appearance of your software

Many window-based applications contain several window elements in addition to the basic messages you receive. These may include toolbars, status bars, folder lists and pop-up formatting aids. Some are very useful, others you might find a waste of space. Once you have been using your e-mail software for a while, you will get to know which you use, and which you would prefer to hide: if you use someone else's computer, you might find they have certain items hidden that you would prefer to show. It's all a matter of personal taste. Most applications now allow you to tailor your view of these items, to personalise your software to suit your exact requirements, and allow you to display items permanently or select them only when you need to use them.

In Microsoft® Outlook Express, you do this by selecting **Layout** from the **View** menu. This displays a list of items, which you can click on or off. If you are not sure what an item is, or where it appears, just click it off and select **OK** to see what has disappeared – you can easily switch it back on again.

Other display options

There are several other display options offered by mainstream e-mail software, but as these vary from one product to another and are not available to all, they are not described in this book. You should refer to your user manual or online help for further information on these options.

CHAPTER 5

Sending e-mail

Now you are ready to start sending messages! In this chapter we look at how to write and send an e-mail message.

Remember that there are many different e-mail products available, so the examples in this chapter, taken from Microsoft® Outlook Express and MSN™ Hotmail®, might not precisely resemble what you see on your screen. The names of functions might be different or items might appear in a different order. However, most e-mail products offer similar functions, so it should be easy to find what you need. The appendix *Alternative names for e-mail functions* lists the names of the functions to use in some other e-mail software. If your product is not listed, or if you get stuck, consult the online help for your product by pressing F1 or selecting the **Help** menu.

Don't forget

Before you start to write, remember:

- If you have to pay for telephone usage, write your messages offline, to reduce your telephone costs. If your e-mail product prompts you to connect when you start it up, just select the option to work offline to continue without logging in.

- If you have to connect to send messages, send them in batches. If you have several messages to send, write them all and then connect, don't connect and send each one individually.

- Check addresses before you send. If you don't, and you get an address wrong, the message may be returned to you, or it may even go to someone else – this is especially important if you are sending to an address like bobjones9375@isp.com as there are probably at least 9374 other users out there named Bob Jones.

- Use plain text unless you know your recipient can view HTML-encoded messages.

- Compress any attachments over 60Kb before sending.

- Be aware of netiquette (see *Observing netiquette* on page 49).

- Don't send anything confidential over public connections (that is, outside your organisation).

Writing an e-mail message

How you start writing an e-mail message depends on whether it is a new message or a reply to an existing message. First we look at how to write a brand new message.

Starting a new message

This is the most basic function of all e-mail software. In most applications the function is called **New**, **New Mail** or **New Message**, in some, **Compose** or **Start Message**. It appears on a menu and often also as a button on a toolbar. For example, in Microsoft® Outlook Express it is called **New**, and appears both as the first button on the toolbar and the first item on the first menu, **File**. In MSN™ Hotmail®, it is called **Compose**, and appears on the menubar.

In some software, such as Microsoft® Outlook Express, you are prompted to select a 'paper' or 'stationery' style when you select **New**; as this is not offered by all software we shall ignore it for now, and discuss it later in the book.

Whatever the name of the function in your e-mail software that allows you to create a new message, when you select it a window will appear containing entry boxes (fields) similar to the ones shown in the example from Microsoft® Outlook Express in Figure 22.

Your own address appears automatically in the **From** box, although if you have more than one address, you might need to select the correct one by clicking on the down arrow to the right of this box. (Note that the free e-mail sites on the Internet, to which you need to log in using the correct address and password before composing your message, often do not show the sender details at all.)

Figure 22: A typical e-mail message window

You will need to type or select the remaining information:

- Type the e-mail address of the recipient (bob_jones@ isp.co.uk in the above example) in the **To** box, or select it from the address book if you have created an entry for this person. If your address book has a 'nickname' function, you can simply type the start of the nickname and the software will complete it automatically, inserting the correct e-mail address for you.

- There is usually a separate area for the e-mail addresses of anyone else who needs a copy . In the example, this is the **Cc** box; there may also be a **Bcc** box for 'blind' copies. Type the address, or select it from the address book.

- Type a subject or title for your message in the **Subject** box. If referring to previous correspondence, use the same subject.

- Type your message in the main text box. Remember to include your name and e-mail address at the end of the message, to make it easier for the person to reply.

- To attach an image or other file, select the **Attach** function and specify the location of the file. Further information on attachments is given later in this chapter.

Once you have composed and checked your e-mail, you are ready to send it. Remember, if you pay for your telephone usage and have several messages to send it is cheaper to write them all first, then send the whole batch at once.

Saving draft messages

Sometimes you might start to write an e-mail message and not have the time, or all the information to hand, to allow you to finish and send it at that time. Your e-mail software should have the option of saving the message as a draft, and of sending now or later; refer to the documentation if it is not clear how to do this. In Microsoft® Outlook Express, you select **Save** from the **File** menu to save the message in your Drafts folder (this helps to prevent you sending it by mistake, if you have further information to add), or **Send later** from the same menu if you are ready to send your message, but don't want to connect yet.

If you save a message as a draft, you can complete it later by selecting it from the Drafts folder, editing it as required and then sending it in the usual way. You can usually also save the message in other common formats for use with word-processing or other software.

Replying to messages

In order to reply to a message or forward it on to another e-mail user, you obviously need to have received and read the message, so we look at how to do this in the next chapter. See *Replying to and forwarding messages*, staring on page 91, for details. At this point, it will suffice to say that in general you do not reply to a message by writing a new message using the New Message function described above.

Attaching files to your messages

There are a number of questions to consider before sending a file to another e-mail user:

- Does the recipient know what the file is and how to handle it?

- Does the recipient have the required software to run the file?

- How large is the file?

Remember that unsolicited mail is a prime source of virus infection. Always describe an attachment fully in the text of your message, and never send an attachment without supporting text, even if you have already arranged to send it. (Similarly, view incoming messages like this with extreme caution, even if you know the sender: see *Handling attachments* on page 88 for further guidance on receiving attachments.)

As part of your description, include:

- The name of the file.

- The file type.

- What application is required to open or run the attachment.

- Any further details, such as whether it is compressed, or if a particular version of software is required.

Repeat this for each attached file unless the bulk of the information is the same for each. For example, if you are sending ten spreadsheets named 'finance1.xls' through 'finance10.xls' you can simply refer to them as finance*.xls, and the remaining information will apply to all.

If the attachment requires particularly obscure software, or a version that is no longer available, and you know that your recipient does not have this, you might wish to explain how to obtain it. Generally, though, it is best to find a common format that both of you are likely to have available. Remember that you should never send copies of licensed software to another person as this infringes licence agreements and could leave you liable to prosecution under copyright law.

Always scan outgoing attachments for possible virus infection. If you unwittingly send on a file containing a virus, you could be responsible for damaging your recipient's computer, or even destroying it completely. Do not think that, because your own computer has not been infected with a virus, all your files are virus-free: some viruses lurk, like some diseases – you can be a carrier without becoming infected. A good virus detection package will pick up such viruses and alert you to their existence: some will even remove the virus, resolving the problem for you. A list of sites offering virus detection software is provided in the appendix *Useful Internet addresses*.

Compressing files

Compressing or zipping a file re-codes it in a format that reduces the amount of disk space it occupies, and thus also reduces the time required to send and download it via e-mail. You should always compress or zip large files before sending, to minimise the cost of transmission and the risk of the file becoming lost or *corrupted*. This is particularly important where telephone lines or modem speeds are slow, as it can take a long time to upload or download a file. You should never send large files unsolicited and uncompressed to another person; it will simply annoy them to spend time downloading a message that might not interest them, and they might respond by adding you to their Blocked Senders list (See the section *Filtering e-mail,* starting on page 66, for details.)

There are several compression utilities available; one or more may be pre-installed on your computer. If not, you can obtain *shareware* or *freeware* versions on the Internet (see the appendix *Useful Internet addresses* for some examples). The most commonly used for Windows®-based products are WinZip and PKzip. Different utilities are required for Macintosh and other operating systems such as AIX and Linux.

It is worth obtaining a suitable zip program even if you don't send many attachments, as almost all software available for download from the Internet is provided in compressed format. Not only is less space needed to store the files and less time/cost incurred in downloading them, but also all the files required by an application are held together in one package, so it is much easier to download.

Remember that, in most cases, if you compress an attachment, the recipient will need the same software to uncompress or unzip it. This is why you should always explain which program you used in the accompanying message. Some zip programs offer a self-extracting facility, that zips your files into a program, which, when selected, unpacks all the files automatically.

Splitting large messages or attachments

Many servers, particularly those used for newsgroups, limit the size of messages you can send and receive. This limit may be as low as one megabyte (1Mb) per message, including all attached files. While this may seem huge if you only send short text messages, just try attaching the occasional graphic, word-processed file or spreadsheet and you will see it is not too difficult to approach this limit, especially if you use colour or fancy fonts. Even if you compress the files, you may still exceed the limit.

To get around this problem, many e-mail products now offer the option of splitting large messages or files into smaller ones when you send them. When the group of messages is received at the recipient's server, their mail program recombines them into one message. This allows the message to move more quickly through the system, without being rejected at any gateway, and to arrive at its destination uncorrupted.

Note, however, that this does not always work across operating systems: for example, if you use this option to split files you are sending from a PC to a Macintosh, they often arrive in pieces, especially if one of the servers along the route did not receive all the pieces at once.

To set file splitting in Microsoft® Outlook Express, select **Properties** from the **Mail** page of the **Accounts** notebook (display this by selecting **Accounts** from the **Tools** menu). Select the **Advanced** page tab and click the checkbox in the **Sending** area, specifying the maximum size for each chunk of your message, as required by the server.

Alternatives to attachments

One final word on attachments: don't send them unnecessarily. If the files are stored somewhere to which your recipient has easy access, such as a shared network drive, just provide the details in your message – if on a web server, list the URL, or address, of the file: if on a shared drive, show the file location. This reduces the disk space required to store your message on the server and the recipient's computer, and helps to maintain optimum speed of transmission and receipt.

Sending your messages

When you are ready to send your messages, use the connection function of your product to dial the ISP's server and transmit your messages. This may be called **Connect** or **Send Mail**. When you select this you are prompted to enter your name or e-mail address and password, which are sent to the server to check your identity. Your software may automatically send the files, or you might have to specifically ask it to do so: it might receive files at the same time, or you might have to tell it to do so. Unfortunately each e-mail application is different, so it is not possible to be specific here. Most software shows a progress indicator while sending, to give you some idea of how many items are being sent and how long it is taking to send each one. Figure 23 shows how this might look.

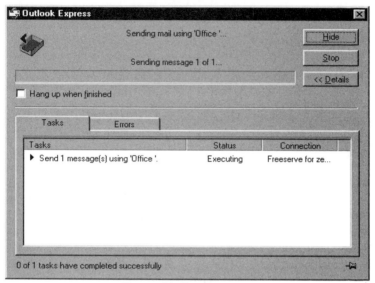

Figure 23: Sending mail

Once an e-mail has been despatched a copy is filed in a Sent or Sent items folder, for you to retrieve later if you wish. This copy contains the date and time of transmission for your records. With some software, and particularly with free e-mail Internet sites, you may have to specify that you want a copy saved, so check first before you send an important document.

Some e-mail software automatically disconnects, ending the phone connection, when all items have been sent and/or received. Others allow you to specify whether you wish to keep the line open: in Microsoft® Outlook Express, for example, you can do this from the **Connection** page of the **Options** notebook (select **Options** from the **Tools** menu to display this) or by clicking the checkbox in the window shown in Figure 23.

Other send options

There are a number of advanced options that may be provided by your software, but are not available on all systems. These options, including message security and encryption features, are likely to be of interest mostly to business users. Some of those most widely available are described in the chapter *E-mail allsorts*, starting on page 105.

CHAPTER 6

Receiving e-mail

Expecting a message? In this chapter we look at how to receive mail, reply to and forward received messages, and file or delete them. We also discover what to do with files sent to you as e-mail attachments.

There are many different e-mail programs available, so the examples in this chapter may not look exactly like those you see on your screen. The names of functions may be different or items may appear in a different order. However, all e-mail programs offer similar functions, so it should be easy to find what you need. If you get stuck, consult the online help for your product by pressing F1 or selecting the **Help** menu option.

Some questions answered

Receiving mail is very simple, but there are a number of questions that often arise. Let's deal with these 'frequently asked questions', or FAQs, first.

How do I know when a message is waiting?

This primarily depends on your e-mail set-up. If you are working in a company where mail is sent via an intranet, your machine may beep when a new message arrives, or you may see a 'new message' indicator on your screen. If you use e-mail at home or have to connect via a phone line, you will not know whether messages have been sent to you until you have dialled in and ask to receive them. This can be irritating, as you might connect, find you have no messages, and disconnect, only for six messages to arrive within minutes, which you only find out about when you next connect. How often you dial in to receive your mail is up to you: if you intend to use e-mail for work in any sense, you will need to dial in at least once a day or risk potential customers going elsewhere due to the lack of a response. If you do not pay for your Internet telephone usage, of course, you could stay connected all day. Whether you do or not will primarily depend on whether you have an alternative line or use the same line for phone or fax as well as the computer, and whether you are concerned that others may be able to access information on your own computer while you are online.

Can I automatically receive messages if I use a dial-up connection?

Some software has an option to connect automatically, and this requires you to save your password so the server does not need to request it. If you work alone, or are meticulous about locking up your screen with a passworded screensaver each time you leave your desk, and if you need to check your mail frequently, this is a possible solution. Otherwise, it is recommended that you do not use this feature as, quite apart from the cost of the calls, it is not secure: anyone with access to your PC could read your mail, and send mail from your account, in your absence.

If you do want to use automatic connection, and are using Microsoft® Outlook Express:

1 Select **Options** from the **Tools** menu to display the **Options** notebook and select the **General** page.

2 Select the checkbox next to **Check for new messages every ... minutes** and specify how often you want your mail to be downloaded.

3 Select **Connect even when working offline** from the drop-down list below.

You will need to ensure that your connection settings automatically supply your password, otherwise you will be prompted to specify this each time the computer tries to connect to the network.

Can I refuse to accept mail?

Once a message has been sent to you, you cannot choose not to receive it, unless the sender is on your Blocked Senders list (see *Filtering e-mail*, starting on page 66, for details). Neither can you change the order in which items are received, although they are downloaded according to priority: the sender of a message can specify a higher priority for an item if it is particularly urgent (see the chapter *E-mail allsorts*).

One of the most irritating things about e-mail is that you usually don't know what you're receiving until it has finally downloaded. It can be infuriating to wait 20 minutes for three files to download, only to find that the first one, which took 95% of the download time, was a message forwarded to 30 different people, containing a series of full-colour graphics in which you have no interest. Unfortunately, there is not much you can do about this, other than politely suggesting to the sender that you would prefer them not to send such items unless they first compress them and describe them in their message; blame the slowness of your connection if you need an excuse.

Now these FAQs are resolved, let's look at how to receive and handle messages.

Receiving mail

This is simple. You just select the option in your e-mail software named **Receive** or **Receive mail**, or even **Check for new mail** or **Refresh**, dial in if you need to, and wait for the messages to drop into your inbox. Most e-mail software displays a progress indicator while this is happening; it may look something like the one in Figure 23 on page 84, but with 'Receiving' in place of 'Sending'.

When messages arrive in your inbox, they are usually highlighted in some way to indicate that they have not yet been read. In Microsoft® Outlook Express, for example, unread messages appear in bold. An example is shown in Figure 24.

Notice how, when an unread message is filed, the folder in which it is stored is highlighted in the folders list, with the number of unread messages shown. This is one of the main benefits of automatic filing: rather than having an inbox with 46 new messages, you can instantly see what the messages are about (although the preciseness of this depends on the definition of your message rules). See the section *Automating your filing with rules and filters* on page 69 for more details on message rules.

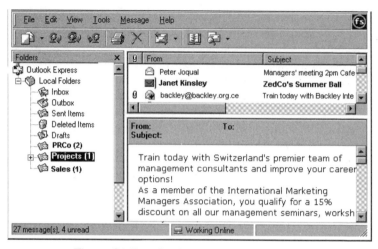

Figure 24: Received and unread messages

Reading a received message

Some e-mail software allows you to preview messages in an area of the main window, so you can scan your messages and do not have to double-click to open a separate window for each one. For example, in Microsoft® Outlook Express, as shown in Figure 24, the preview pane is the lower right-hand side of the window, where the selected message (about training in this example) can be viewed. You can choose whether or not to display the preview window in most cases and some software allows a choice of where to display it. If your software does not provide a preview facility, you will need to open each message in turn to view its content.

To view information about a received message, such as the date and time at which it was sent, you need to check the message header. See *The message header* on page 113 for details of how to use the header information.

Handling attachments

Attachments are computer files that are sent as part of an e-mail message. They are usually indicated on your screen by a paperclip or document button next to the message. In some e-mail programs attachments may be viewed inline as part of the message rather than as a separate file, but this usually applies only to HTML-enabled software.

Attachments come in all forms. If your correspondence is primarily personal, the attachments you receive may vary from word-processed documents to family photos, sound and video recordings – it all depends on the resources available to your correspondents, of course. If you view messages as plain text, and someone sends you a message in HTML, the HTML version will appear as an attachment to the plain text message with the file extension .htm or .rtf.

If you are in business, you might receive files of many types, including spreadsheets, word-processed documents, programs, databases and graphics. You might even receive faxes as attachments to e-mail, if you use an electronic fax manager.

It is difficult to be specific in how to handle attachments. However, there is some advice that applies to everybody and to all attachment types: this concerns computer viruses.

Attachments and computer viruses

Computer viruses are one of the biggest problems with e-mail today (see the section *Avoiding computer viruses* on page 47). They are easily spread by e-mail, most commonly via attachments. There are some simple guidelines to help you prevent damage through computer viruses:

- First, obtain, install and use a good virus detection package. Use it daily, preferably by adding it to your start-up sequence, and update it regularly. This is essential to protect the data on your computer from potential virus damage: if the package captures only one virus sent to you via e-mail or on a disk, it will have paid for itself many times over. The appendix *Useful Internet addresses* contains some addresses for websites offering virus detection software. Be aware, however, that no virus detection package will guarantee protection against every virus; for protection to be available, a virus must be known about and an antidote be made available and downloaded to your computer. Antidotes are usually available fairly quickly, but it is up to you to download them in order to protect your system.

- If you receive an e-mail containing an attachment, and you do not know the sender, DO NOT OPEN IT as it might contain a virus. Unsolicited mail is one of the easiest and most frequent ways to propagate viruses that cause complete destruction of your hard drive and everything on it, and sometimes this includes further propagation of the virus via your e-mail contacts information to other users. Luckily most such viruses can only be activated when the attachment in which they are contained is opened by the recipient – so don't! Try to contact the sender first to check what the attachment contains.

• Even if you do know the sender, it is wise to take care with attachments, especially if they are not mentioned in the message. Some viruses operate by attaching themselves invisibly to e-mail messages as they circulate through the network. Be particularly wary of attachments with a .exe or .cmd extension as this indicates a program or command. Check with the sender by another means if you are unsure of the validity of an attachment.

• If you suspect your machine may have become infected with a virus, do not connect to the Internet to send or receive mail until you are certain that the virus has been removed. To do so could result in the virus spreading further, to any or all of your e-mail contacts.

Opening and saving attachments

If you are certain that an attachment is valid, and does not contain a virus, you usually have two options:

• You can open the file without storing it on your machine.

• You can save the attachment to a hard/network drive.

To do this, select the relevant menu option (usually called **Open attachment** or **Save attachment** and located on the **File** menu), or select the attachment button next to the message to display the options and the names of the attached files.

For example, in Microsoft® Outlook Express, you can high-light the message in the list to display it in the preview pane, then select the paperclip button that appears at the top right of the preview pane to display a drop-down list of the attached files. Select a filename to open that file. The last item on this list is an option to save the attachments.

If opening an attachment, you might be prompted to select which application to use: this will depend on the file extension and whether you have associated this file type with a program on your computer (see your operating system documentation for details of how to do this).

If saving an attachment, you will be prompted to specify a location for the file.

Viewing attachments inline

The problem with viewing inline is that an attachment has to be opened before it can appear, and as previously mentioned, opening attachments can be dangerous. However, if you have good virus detection software and if you prefer to view your attachments as part of the message there is usually an option to do so. It might also depend on the option selected by the sender: if he or she cuts and pastes a graphic directly into the text entry area, it will probably appear inline in your inbox, whereas if they use the attach feature to send it as an attached file, it will not.

There is no obvious way to enable or prevent the inline display of attachments in Microsoft® Outlook Express: if you are sent a message with inline graphics, for example, they appear as such automatically. In other software, such as Netscape® Messenger™, there are menu options you can select to view attachments inline or as attached files.

Replying to and forwarding messages

First, let's resolve one frequently asked question, or FAQ:

What's the difference between a reply and a forward?

It is determined by where, or to whom, you are sending the message. If someone has sent you a message that you think might be useful to someone else, you may *forward* that message on to that third person. If you are providing information to the person who *sent* the message, usually about the content of the message, that is a *reply*. Of course, you may respond to a message you have received by forwarding the contents of a different message to the sender, but in e-mail terms, that is not the same as a reply. It is also not considered a reply if you start a new message to respond to the sender. Although it seems perfectly reasonable to do so, it is annoying if your recipient uses threaded display (see *Grouping messages by subject* on page 74), as the response does not appear correctly in the display.

Other than this, there is no mystery to the reply and forward functions. With most software, to reply, you select a **Reply** button, or select **Reply** from a menu, and to forward, you select **Forward**. If you are not sure which button is which for your software, check the online help or manual.

When you select one of these options, a window appears to allow you to write your message. Figure 25 shows what this looks like in Microsoft® Outlook Express.

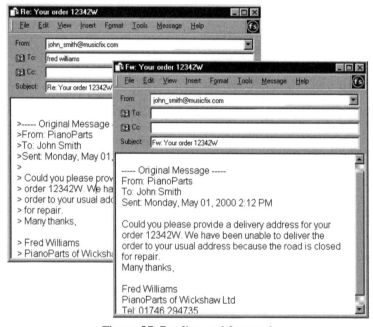

Figure 25: Replies and forwards

As you can see, they look very similar. In fact the only obvious differences in this example are:

• For a reply, the **To** box already contains a name (of the person who sent the original message); for a forward it is blank.

• For a reply, the **Subject** line shows the subject of the original message prefixed by Re:, while a forward shows Fw:

- For a reply, the message to which you are replying is shown and prefixed with a chevron (>); in a forward no prefix is used.

Otherwise you treat the two the same, and the same as any new message. You write your text, including quotes from the original if required (see below), and click on **Send** to send it.

Quoting from a message

When you first select **Reply** or **Forward**, you might find that the content of the original message appears in the window, as shown in Figure 25. This allows you to quote part or all of the original message to your recipient.

I say 'you might' because it is not always the default to show this information; some e-mail products do, others do not. Some software, such as Lotus Notes®, offers you the choice of replying or replying with history; the second is used when you want to quote. For other software, you may have to set an option to quote the original message automatically. In Microsoft® Outlook Express, you change this setting by selecting **Options** from the **Tools** menu, selecting the **Send** page, and changing the following:

- If you write in plain text, select the **Plain text** settings in the **Mail settings** section, and click on the checkbox **Indent the original text with**. You can select one of several characters here, but the most commonly used is the chevron.

- If you send mail in HTML, select the **HTML settings** button in the **Mail settings** section and click on the checkbox **Indent message on reply**. Usually a vertical line is used to indicate quoted text in HTML, in place of the chevron.

- If you send mail to newsgroups, repeat the above for the **News settings** section.

Considerations for replies and forwards

You will often receive messages containing quoted or forwarded items, and sometimes, when the item has been forwarded many times, the number of headers, signatures and odd lines of text can make the message almost unreadable. Usually the most important part – the original message – is to be found at the end of the message, but this is not always the case, so it is easy to miss the relevant point of such a message.

It is therefore good practice to quote only those parts of a message that are relevant – you can delete the others from your reply or forward in the same way as you would delete any other text. Indicate where you have deleted text by inserting the following on the line before and after the quote:

<snipped>
or
<snipped by Bob Jones>

Business netiquette suggests you should always retain the names of other forwarders, so as not to infringe copyright or submit yourself to claims of plagiarism, and in business this can be quite strictly enforced. In informal or personal mail, however, this is less important. If, like me, you are bombarded with forwarded messages containing jokes and scanned images – sent via half the world's e-mail users, it sometimes seems – you'd probably prefer to not to have to scroll through the names of all the people who'd seen it first just to get your laughs.

It is really up to you whether to add your own introduction to a message you are forwarding. You do not have to add anything, as your e-mail address appears at the top of the message anyway, and many people do not – particularly with circulated humour and images. This is rather like sending flowers without a message: the recipient knows which florist sent them, and can find out who ordered them, but it's the message that makes it personal.

Filing received messages

If you do not use automatic filing, as described in *Automating your filing with rules and filters* on page 69, but have several folders set up for your mail, you will probably want to move messages from one folder to another in order to file them appropriately. To do this, you usually have two options:

- With the folder list displayed, select the message in the list and *drag* it (holding down the mouse button) on top of the folder you require, then *drop* it (release the mouse button) to move it to that folder.

- Select the message and select a menu option to move it. This option is usually called **Move** or **Transfer**; in Microsoft® Outlook Express it is called **Move to folder** and appears on the **Edit** menu.

Deleting messages

It is a good idea to delete messages you no longer require, primarily to prevent your hard disk from filling up and to help your e-mail application to run more quickly.

Most e-mail software contains a fail-safe deletion system; when you ask to delete a message it is placed into a **Deleted items** folder, rather than being erased immediately. (This works the same way as the Recycle bin in Windows®.) You can then empty this folder as often as you wish – obviously until you empty it, the messages are still clogging up your system.

To delete a message, first select it, then you can usually do one of the following (depending on your software):

- Hit the **Delete** key.

- Click on a **Delete** button.

- Select a **Delete** menu option (usually on the **Edit** menu).

If you delete a message by mistake, just open the **Deleted items** folder, select the message and move it back to the folder you require (see *Filing received messages* above).

In Microsoft® Outlook Express, if you want to discard deleted items automatically each time you exit the program, do the following:

1 Open the **Maintenance** page of the **Options** notebook (select **Options** from the **Tools** menu to display this).

2 Click on the first checkbox (**Empty messages ...**) and then click **OK**.

CHAPTER 7

Communicating with others

We now know that e-mail can be used to send personal or business-related messages from one person to another. But it can also be used for much more. Most of the subjects discussed in this chapter are of particular interest to business users, but others may find this information useful too, particularly to find other people with similar interests or to find solutions to problems. Most of these require the use of an Internet browser, such as Microsoft® Internet Explorer or Netscape® Communicator™, in addition to your e-mail software.

Using bulletin boards (BBS)

A bulletin board service, or BBS, is a computer that is linked to the Internet to allow users to share or exchange messages or other files: the electronic equivalent of a pinboard in the corridor or the postcards in a newsagent's window. Some bulletin boards are devoted to discussions on specific topics, while others provide a more general service. There are currently many thousands of different bulletin boards available world-wide: mostly the discussions are conducted in English, but some are specific to other languages.

There are bulletin boards available for almost any subject you can think of, from industrial and technical information exchanges to stamp collecting, obscure sports, archaeology and cookery, as well as the ever popular 'adult' boards. Most bulletin board services are free of charge and available to anyone, but some, particularly professional groups, charge a membership or usage fee, often to cover the cost of administration and any charges made by the service provider for hosting the service.

Bulletin boards developed separately from the world-wide web, and for some you might still need to connect to the BBS computer directly, rather than through your Internet connection. However, most bulletin boards these days have websites at which you can connect or, if not, obtain the necessary software to get connected.

An official bulletin board magazine, *Boardwatch*, is available on the Internet and provides useful tips on how to use and find bulletin boards to suit you. You can find the latest version of the magazine at www.boardwatch.com

Using newsgroups

Newsgroups, sometimes called *forums* or *fora*, are basically online discussion groups and, like bulletin boards, there are many thousands of them, covering every conceivable interest. Individual e-mail users join newsgroups to read, request and supply information on a topic, supplied in *postings*, which is just another name for e-mail messages, when they are sent to a communal service like this. To view messages on and post (send) messages to a newsgroup, you need a newsreader program that directs you to the appropriate server. Most ISPs now provide newsreaders for major newsgroups as part of their web connection software. With this software, you can post messages to existing newsgroups, respond to previous posts, and create new newsgroups.

Most newsgroups concentrate their discussions on a particular subject. Discussions are formed from individual notes written by e-mail users, which are sent to a specific e-mail address representing a news server. On receipt at the server, the message is copied to news servers world-wide using a technology called Usenet, and subscribers to that newsgroup receive a copy of the message in their inbox when they next check their e-mail. If you don't want to be swamped by messages in your inbox, you can usually read and post to a newsgroup without subscribing: you then need to connect to a particular server to view the postings in a list format.

Newsgroup names

The first part of a newsgroup's name indicates the major subject category and the rest indicates sub-categories: rather like some web addresses. For example, some of the major subject categories are:

alt	alternative
bus	business
comp	computers
news	news
rec	recreational
sci	science
soc	social/society

Some newsgroup names start with a country code (for example, uk, za) if their content is specific to one country. Others start with the name of the newsgroup provider, for example zetnet, claranet, or telnet.

Here are some examples of newsgroup names:

- **news.freeserve.net** is a 'news' newsgroup provided by the ISP Freeserve (in the UK).

- **alt.fan.nicole.kidman** provides news and gossip for fans of this actress.

- **fr.sci.psychologie** is a French newsgroup on psychology (with discussions conducted in French).

- **japan.pets.dogs.breed** provides information for Japanese dog-breeders.

- **sci.optics.fiber** is a forum for discussion on fibre optic technology.

- **sdnet.sports** provides details of sports in the San Diego area.

- **soc.men** discusses issues related to men and their problems (**soc.women** does the same for women).

- **uk.rec.motorcycles** is a UK-based newsgroup for those interested in recreational motorcycling.

- **za.org.cssa** is the newsgroup for the Computer Society of South Africa.

Some companies provide support for their products via newsgroups, and in this case the company name is usually the first part of the newsgroup name, for example:

novell.netware3.installupgrades
symantec.support.win95
usa-today.money
zippo.announce

Finding newsgroups

How you go about finding a newsgroup depends on which e-mail software you use, and whether your ISP provides you with the newsreader software to allow you to access newsgroups. You can easily see whether or not you have access to newsgroups: in the main window of your e-mail software, there should be an item such as news.isp.co.uk, with a different icon to that used for folders, or an option called **News** or **Newsgroups**. Some e-mail software, such as Netscape® Messenger™, provides a separate window for viewing newsgroups (you can open this from the **Window** menu of the main Netscape® Messenger™ window).

If you use Microsoft® Outlook Express with a connection to an ISP providing newsgroup information, you will find a newsgroup item in your folder list, at the same level as your Local Folders list. This may be called, for example, news.isp.net (notice there are no @ signs in newsgroup names). If you select this item, a list of available newsgroups will be displayed in the main part of the window, as shown in Figure 26.

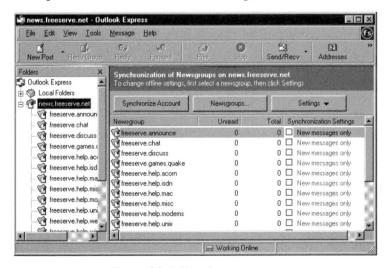

Figure 26: A list of newsgroups

You can select further newsgroups by clicking on the **Newsgroups** button at the top of this list.

To view the postings of a newsgroup since you last viewed it, you use the synchronisation feature. Read the documentation that came with your e-mail software to find out how to do this, as it varies from one product to another.

Posting messages to newsgroups

Before posting to a newsgroup, learn basic netiquette (some of which is described in the chapter *The basics of e-mail*, starting on page 49) and become familiar with the content of the newsgroup and the style of its postings. Most newsgroups have specific sets of rules relating to the format and content of messages, and provide a list of FAQs to prevent the same questions being asked repeatedly. Most expect postings in fairly informal language, but it is wise to read first and adapt your style to suit.

Some newsgroups are moderated by a designated person who decides which postings to allow or to remove: these often show 'moderated' or 'mod' as part of the name. However, most newsgroups are unmoderated.

Subscribing to lists

A mailing list, or subscription list, is a basically a list of e-mail users who receive periodic e-mails on a particular topic, distributed from a central source. They are a popular way for e-mail users to keep informed on subjects in which they have a particular interest. Many corporations are now using them as a marketing and customer relations aid.

There are two main types of list:

- An announce list is like a traditional newsletter, sent from one source with no feedback from its recipients.

- A discussion list is more like a newsgroup: an exchange of messages between subscribers.

How a list operates depends on its size, and the requirements of its readers. Most lists with more than 1,000 subscribers offer a discussion facility, although this might be separate from the original announce list.

Types of list

There are many thousands of lists available, covering subjects as diverse as you can imagine. Some of these are public lists, available to anyone; most are private, with access limited to specific, invited members. You can often request membership of a private list by contacting its webmaster, or list owner: the relevant e-mail address or contact information is usually provided on the organisation's website or directory listing.

As with newsgroups, some lists are moderated or monitored. On unmoderated lists you can post almost anything, as no one checks or monitors the messages; on a moderated list, a designated person reads and often edits or deletes messages before distribution, to ensure they are appropriate for the list and to keep the volume of messages manageable. The moderator may decide, for example, that a long-running discussion on a list warrants its own list, or its own FAQ listing.

Gated lists work rather differently to other lists. These are often high-volume lists, with many postings per day, and to make it easier to sort the relevant from the irrelevant, they are operated via a newsgroup, allowing you to read their content with a newsreader rather than downloading all the individual messages via your e-mail software.

Many lists allow you to request a daily or weekly digest of content, rather than individual messages. In a digest, all the messages received in that period are condensed into a single message: in some cases they are further edited and condensed to provide only an outline of the various discussions, with links to the individual messages for further details. This is especially handy if you only want to scan the content of a list for anything of particular interest, and don't want to wade through the inevitable chats, quips, comments and 'me too' messages that proliferate on newsgroups. If your software offers a search facility (in Windows® software, usually activated by selecting Ctrl+F, or Alt+F), you can scan such digests quickly by looking only for words that might catch your interest.

Finding and subscribing to a list

There are many thousands of lists available, so finding one to suit you should not be too difficult. There are several websites that allow you to search for lists by title or subject, and some supply brief details of the group and how to subscribe to it.

Some of these are listed in the appendix *Useful Internet addresses*.

You can find further information on the use of mailing lists at any of the Internet encyclopaedia sites listed in that appendix.

Starting your own list

If you have a particular interest that you think others may share, you can start your own list. Often your ISP will help you set up a list and maintain it on the ISP server: if yours doesn't offer this service, try another one. You will probably have to pay for this service. If you want a good response, it is wise to check first to ensure that there is not already a well-used list or newsgroup serving this particular interest: it is usually difficult to persuade people to leave one list to use another, or even to read both. However, if your list will offer a specialism, for example, if you have an interest in art deco jewellery and existing lists and newsgroups deal only with collectable jewellery or art deco artefacts in general, you might have the basis for a new list and advertising the new service on the existing lists and groups (if this is allowed by their owners) would be a productive way to attract attention to it.

The first few days and weeks of a list can be trying. Think of it as a party where nobody knows anyone else but they share a common interest; it can take some time for it to get going and for a while at least will be dominated by the self-important. Those with a casual interest or less qualified opinions may lurk – reading the list content avidly but not participating. Information may flow in fits and starts, with hundreds of messages one day and three the next. Questions may go unanswered while one particular issue strays 'off-topic' and threatens to change the whole nature of the list. Often your job as list owner will be to guide such discussions back to more relevance, or suggest that the participants take it 'off-list', continuing the discussion by e-mailing each other privately rather than through the list. You may sometimes feel the need to 'seed' questions (asking a question to which you don't particularly want or need to know the answer, but which will generate much discussion) to bolster flagging interest or to bring a particular issue to the fore.

Running a list can be fun, but expect to take often unwarranted blame for problems such as messages not appearing or taking a long time to appear on the list. (This is usually due to server problems that are outside your control.) Deal with frequent posters of irrelevant or inappropriate content politely but firmly, and preferably privately rather than via the list: if their interference reaches an unacceptable level and they do not respond to polite requests to desist, use the blocking features to prevent them from posting further. Provide a guidance document listing what is and is not acceptable, and keep list users informed of any changes, such as the creation of new lists to serve sub-groups or a change in the location or registration details for a list. Overall, enjoy yourself and don't exert too much control: you can make new friends and gain valuable information through lists, but nobody likes to feel they are being censored or 'nannied' too often.

Using chatrooms

Chatrooms are basically interactive websites that allow you to send and receive messages almost instantaneously, just like a real-life conversation. They do not strictly involve the use of e-mail but are often run in conjunction with BBS or newsgroups using the Internet. They use a technology called IRC (Internet Relay Chat) which requires you to download a program from the host website before you can start to chat online. There are many established chat sites that are open all hours, while others are provided for a specific period on a host website, to allow people to send questions to and chat to a particular person; you may have seen such chats on TV programmes. They are useful for broadcasters as they are far easier to control and censor than the traditional phone-in, which often attracts a lot of 'crank' callers. Chatrooms do too, but it is easy to ignore or discard displayed messages, while cutting off a broadcast telephone caller in mid-sentence may be justified, but often seems rude.

Most chat users use a nickname rather than their own details, and although honesty is encouraged, in theory anyone could masquerade as someone else. This has led to allegations that chatrooms are unsafe and unhealthy, especially for children who could be led into giving out personal details or arranging meetings with someone they have never met. It is certainly wise to exercise some control or monitoring of children's use of chatrooms. However, if you are sensible, some chatrooms can be a lot of harmless fun.

For more information on chatrooms, see the appendix *Useful Internet addresses*. Most ISP sites and search engines also have information on chatrooms and links to chat channels that they support.

Using FTP to send files

If you often need to send or exchange files with other Internet users, you may find it laborious to do so using e-mail attachments. There is an alternative: FTP (File Transfer Protocol) is the simplest way to exchange files between computers on the Internet. FTP is commonly used to transfer website page files from their creator to their server so that everyone on the Internet can access them. It is also frequently used to download programs and files to your computer from other servers: your Internet browser can make FTP requests to download programs you select from a website. You can also use FTP to delete, rename, move and copy files on a server.

Basic FTP support is usually provided as part of your e-mail and Internet software; as functions vary between browsers, check your product's documentation for details of how to use it. If you want customers or other users to be able to use FTP to access your files, you will need to have them stored on a server: your ISP should be able to arrange this.

CHAPTER 8:

E-mail allsorts

This chapter is called 'allsorts' because it contains a mixed bag of topics: discussions on a variety of e-mail features and subjects beyond the mere sending and receiving of messages and files. This includes the use of HTML; digital signatures and message encryption; how to find information about your e-mail messages; how to read foreign e-mail; and the legal implications of e-mail correspondence.

Using HTML in your messages

HTML, or Hypertext Mark-up Language, to give it its full title, is basically a formatting mechanism for text displayed on a computer screen. It is known as the 'language of the Internet' because it is the format used for most web pages and downloadable documents, and it can be used in e-mail messages, if your e-mail software supports it. In its raw or original format, HTML consists of a lot of instructions, or tags, that tell the computer how to display the text. An example of this can be seen in Figure 30 on page 109. If your software can handle HTML, however, you are unlikely to see this format unless you specifically request to do so, as it will automatically convert the tagged text to the display it represents.

A few years ago, in order to produce an HTML document you needed to know the tags and laboriously type them into a plain text document and pass it through a compiler program to produce a document containing the effects you required. Nowadays this is no longer necessary: if writing web pages you can purchase software that allows you simply to drop graphical items on to the page and type text, selecting highlighting and emphasis options as you would in a word processor. If your e-mail software allows you to send HTML messages (and most of the most popular commercial software does), you can do the same, usually by selecting text effects from a toolbar at the top of the message window.

To do this in Microsoft® Outlook Express, select **Rich Text (HTML)** from the **Format** menu in the message window. To set HTML as the default format for messages, go to the main window and select **Options** from the **Tools** menu. Select the **Send** page and click next to the option **HTML**, which appears under **Mail Settings**.

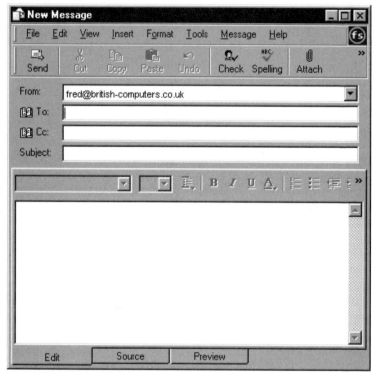

Figure 27: An HTML message window

HTML is certainly more attractive in appearance than plain text. It allows you more freedom in how you lay out your message, and is especially good for tabulated lists or where you need to emphasise words or phrases. Some of the features of HTML that are most commonly used in messages are:

- Bold or italic text
- Underlining

- Colour

- Different sizes of text

- Different fonts (typefaces)

- Bulleted or numbered lists

- Tables

Plain text is very restrictive, not allowing even bold or italics for emphasis, which most computer users are used to from using word-processed documents. However, the big drawback with HTML is that not all users of e-mail have software that can read it.

So when is it acceptable to use HTML? Generally speaking, if you work in an organisation in which all e-mail recipients use the same software, it is safe to use HTML. Even if you are using e-mail from home or your own business, if you know for certain that your recipient uses one of the 'mainstream' e-mail products such as Microsoft® Outlook Express or Netscape® Messenger™, you can use it. But if you are writing to someone who uses less common software, or who uses one of the free e-mail websites (OSPs), it is less certain that they will be able to read it. Most newsgroups and lists prefer people to write in plain text: it takes up less space on the server and is universally readable. However, if you do write an HTML message to a user whose software cannot read HTML they can still see the message; it just loses all its highlighting so items you have emphasised will not appear as such. You can see this in the examples overleaf.

Figure 28 shows an example of a message written in HTML, on one of the 'stationery' backgrounds provided in Outlook Express.

The original of the message shown in Figure 28 also contains coloured text, which adds to the emphasis. There are all kinds of emphasis available with HTML, including blinking text, text that moves across the screen (called a scrolling banner), and background images, as well as the full range of typefaces and styles. But is it worth it? If the recipient's e-mail software doesn't show formatted HTML, all she will see is a plain text version, looking something like Figure 29.

Hi *Angela and Dave*,

! GREAT NEWS !

We are coming to Harare!
John has to visit on a business trip, and we are all coming along for the ride. We all hope we can meet with you, so let us know your plans. Here are ours:

---

* We arrive on 20th Feb and leave on 2nd March

* We are staying at the *Continental Hotel* on Broad Street

* John will be working from 9 to 4 each day except the weekend

---

We're really excited, it's so long since we saw you, I can't wait!

Love *Joan xxx*

Figure 28: A message formatted in HTML

Hi Angela and Dave,

! Great news !

We are coming to Harare!
John has to visit on a business trip, and we are all coming along for the ride. We all hope we can meet with you, so let us know your plans. Here are ours:

----

a.. We arrive on 20th Feb and leave on 2nd March
b.. We are staying at the Continental Hotel on Broad Street
c.. John will be working from 9 to 4 each day except the weekend

----

We're really excited, it's so long since we saw you. I can't wait!

Love Joan xxx

Figure 29: An HTML-encoded message viewed as plain text

Little point then, you may say, in spending all that time and effort adding fancy typefaces and emphasis. At least Angela can read the message: she might be confused by the file attached to it, however, as this would contain the 'raw' or coded HTML source, which, if she had no HTML browser, would open in a word processor looking something like this:

```
<!DOCTYPE HTML PUBLIC "-//W3C//DTD HTML 4.0
Transitional//EN">
<HTML><HEAD>
<META content="text/html; charset=iso-8859-1" http-
equiv=Content-Type><BASE
href="file://C:\Program Files\Common Files\Microsoft
Shared\Stationery\">
<STYLE>BODY {BACKGROUND-COLOR: #ffffff; BACKGROUND-
POSITION: left top; BACKGROUND-REPEAT: repeat-y;
COLOR: #ff9900; FONT-FAMILY: "Comic Sans MS"; FONT-
SIZE: 14pt; FONT-WEIGHT: normal; MARGIN-BOTTOM: 0em;
MARGIN-LEFT: 5em; MARGIN-TOP: 0em}
P.msoNormal {BACKGROUND-COLOR: #ffffff; BACKGROUND-
POSITION: left top; BACKGROUND-REPEAT: repeat-y;
COLOR: #ff9900; FONT-FAMILY: "Comic Sans MS"; FONT-
SIZE: 14pt; FONT-WEIGHT: normal; MARGIN-BOTTOM: 0em;
MARGIN-LEFT: 5em; MARGIN-TOP: 0em}
LI.msoNormal {BACKGROUND-COLOR: #ffffff; BACKGROUND-
POSITION: left top; BACKGROUND-REPEAT: repeat-y;
COLOR: #ff9900; FONT-FAMILY: "Comic Sans MS"; FONT-
```

Figure 30: 'Raw' HTML

Rather unreadable, to say the least, and in fact this is only the top few lines of the file – to show the whole file would take several pages of this book. This is why plain text remains the norm for e-mail communication, at least until HTML-enabled applications are in wider use.

Using stationery

Some e-mail software provides various backgrounds, or 'stationery', on which you can type your message. Some have a border around the edge that give a hand-written feel to personal notes, rather like patterned notepaper; others feature seasonal graphics and a box for you to enter your text. What they all feature is some form of graphical content, so they are unsuitable for sending to people who cannot receive HTML files. They are also mostly unsuitable for business use, although some organisations produce their own stationery background for e-mail messages and these are obviously the exception.

For personal e-mail, however, stationery can add a certain edge to your messages. You can easily view the stationery available to you, and some software allows you to design and add your own backgrounds. In Outlook Express, you select stationery from the drop-down menu that appears when you click the **New Message** icon.

Advanced security options

Security is one of the main considerations for most businesses when purchasing or installing an e-mail system, especially when this is as part of an intranet. If this includes access to the 'outside world' such as the Internet, it is possible that someone unauthorised could read, and possibly alter, data existing on the systems connected to the intranet. This is usually prevented by the use of firewalls, which act as 'gatekeepers' to such systems, allowing only certain data to pass in and out. Firewalls are rather beyond the scope of this book, as they cover more than just e-mail: seek professional advice if you feel you need this level of security. For most users, advanced security extends only to the use of digital signatures or certificates, and, where possible, password-protected attachments.

Proving identity

One of the big problems with e-mail is its non-personal nature. How can you tell for certain whether an e-mail message sent from fred@british-computers.co.uk was actually written by Fred himself? Maybe Fred is ill, and someone else is replying to his mail; maybe his secretary reads his incoming mail and answers items when he is too busy; maybe fred@british-computers.co.uk is actually a shared address, like sales@arrowink.com, and you may never have corresponded with Fred himself at all – indeed Fred may not exist. How would you know? It is remarkably easy to convince someone you are who you are not: we automatically expect a message to come from the person whose name appears at the top. For most personal e-mail, the consequences are not too serious, but how about for business? If you frequently received orders by e-mail from fred@british-computers.co.uk, would it cross your mind that the next order might be the result of fraudulent use of his e-mail address? If you received a message asking you to send a confidential document, and that message came from a person within your organisation that you had not previously dealt with, but whose e-mail address showed them to be working on your intranet (that is, it had the same domain details), would you think twice before sending the information requested? Probably not, yet this is how hackers, and particularly industrial spies, obtain their information: they rely on the innate trust of e-mail users in the infallibility of technology.

So how can you prevent this and prove that you really are who you say you are? One way is to use a digital certificate (sometimes called digital signature or digital ID) on each message.

Getting a digital certificate

Digital certificates are not supported by all e-mail software, so before you read this section, check your product's manuals or online help to see whether you have this facility. Microsoft® Outlook Express and Netscape® Messenger™ support all forms of digital certificate.

Digital certificates offer the most secure way to prove you are who you say you are for e-mail correspondence. They contain information that identifies you personally and can be used to both sign and encrypt messages. They are issued by independent certification organisations, who operate via the Internet: some addresses for these sites are given in the appendix *Useful Internet addresses*. Each is used for a specific mail account or e-mail address, so if you want to send secure mail from more than one address, you will need to apply for an ID for each. To send a digitally encrypted message, you will need the digital certificate of your recipient.

When you first look at some certification sites you may be rather put off by all the technical jargon. Don't be, as this probably relates to the server certification products rather than those required for individual use: look for the link to Personal Certificates (or Class 1 certificates) and this should lead you to the right information. It is generally easy to follow and you can obtain a certificate almost instantly, once you have provided the relevant information in an online form. If you do require further digital protection, say if you are operating a web server, then these sites should have all the information you require.

You will have to pay for obtaining and using a digital certificate, but the cost is fairly low (currently around £8 or US$15 per year). If you send information that could be valuable to others, or that must be proved to have come from you, this is a very economical and safe way to do so.

Sending and receiving digitally certified e-mail

When you have obtained your certificate, you need to decide whether to apply it automatically to all outgoing messages, or just to apply it when needed. Signing a message with your digital certificate indicates to the recipient that the message definitely came from you, and that it was not tampered with en route. It does not, however, protect you against interference from hackers: only encryption can do this. Your recipients do not need to have any additional software themselves in order to read your digitally signed message, unless you wish to encrypt it. In this case, you actually require their digital certificate, as this contains the key to the encryption used.

The easiest way to get someone's digital certificate is to ask him or her to send you a digitally signed message. Details of the certificate then travel with the message and are added to your address book with the user's details. If you cannot ask for this information, go to one of the certification sites and look up the name of your contact in their lists; if their certification was issued by one of the partner companies, you should be able to find it.

Messages that are digitally signed or encrypted appear in your inbox with a different icon to indicate that they are secure. You do not need to open them any differently; your software should automatically recognise and decode them based on the certification information you have stored.

If you send a digitally signed message to someone whose e-mail software cannot handle digital certificates, they should still be able to read your message, but will be unable to reply over a secure link.

Further information on digital certification is available from the certification sites, some of which are listed in the appendix *Useful Internet addresses*.

Encrypting messages

Encryption allows further security on your message by scrambling its content, making it more difficult for a hacker to access and decode it. Generally speaking, you can only encrypt an e-mail message if you have your recipient's digital signature, and their message to you can only be encrypted if they have yours. There is nothing complicated about encryption. You usually need only to select the option in your e-mail software called **Encrypt**. In Microsoft® Outlook Express, you can find this on the **Tools** menu of the message window. If you regularly send digitally signed mail, you can select to encrypt all messages by default. In Outlook Express, you can set this on the **Security** page of the **Options** notebook (select **Options** from the **Tools** menu of the main window to display this).

You do not need to do anything to 'unencrypt' a message: as the digital signature is sent with it this acts as the key and decodes the message when you open or preview it. Most software indicates a message is encrypted by showing a different message icon, often featuring a lock or key.

The message header

Message headers contain all the 'technical' information about an e-mail message and its route from sender to recipient, including details of all the servers and gateways it passes en route, and any encryption or encoding applied to it. Most software hides the message header from immediate view, or shows only part of the information, as it is basically gobbledegook unless you really understand the technicalities. However, should you need to view the header, say to check the time a received message was despatched by the sender, there is usually an option allowing you to do so.

Each e-mail application is different, so use your software's online help to identify the function that allows you to view this information. In Microsoft® Outlook Express, for example, you select the message, click the right mouse button, and select **Properties** from the pop-up menu to view the header information on the **Details** page of the **Properties** notebook.

Earlier in this book, we looked at a message sent from Bob Jones to his brother John in Australia. The header information for this message would look something like this:

```
Reply-To: "Bob Jones" <bob@isp.co.uk>
From: "Bob Jones" <bob@isp.co.uk>
To: "John" <john@reeftours.au>
Subject: Happy Birthday John!
Date: Mon, 27 Mar 2000 09:44:35 +0100
Organization: None
MIME-Version: 1.0
Content-Type: text/plain;
        charset="iso-8859-1"
Content-Transfer-Encoding: 7bit
X-Priority: 3
X-MSMail-Priority: Normal
X-Mailer: Microsoft Outlook Express 5.00.2014.211
X-MimeOLE: Produced By Microsoft MimeOLE V5.00.2014.211
```

Figure 31: Example of message header (sent message)

You can see that it shows the sender and addressee, and the time at which the message was created (the +0100 indicates the time zone, in this case, British Summer Time, one hour ahead of GMT). The 'Organisation' line would show the name of the company, if this were from a business address. The rest of the information relates to the technical aspects of the transmission; how the message was broken down and encoded, what protocols and character set and which version of the mailing software were used – all rather meaningless and unimportant to most users, even experienced ones. If you really need to know what each line means, check with the manufacturer of your e-mail software or look it up on the Internet.

The version above shows what would appear on Bob's computer. On John's computer, at which the message was received, there would be far more information:

```
X-From_: bob_jones@isp.co.uk Thu Dec 02 13:16:08 1999
Envelope-to: john@reeftours.co.au
Delivery-date: Mon, 27 Mar 2000 09:44:35 +0100
Received: from [208.233.96.50] (helo=exclamation.net)
        by mail7.svr.pol.co.uk with smtp (Exim 3.11 #0)
        id 11tW5g-0001sz-00
        for john@reeftours.co.au; Mon, 27 Mar 2000 09:44:35 +0100
Received: from nsl.warnnet.net [208.237.127.220] by exclamation.net with ESMTP
  (SMTPD32-4.03) id A28C4E7C0062; Mon, 27 Mar 2000 21:22:20 EST
Received: by GSSERVER with Internet Mail Service (5.0.1459.44)
        id <X6J655XJ>; Mon, 27 March 2000 21:33:14 +1000
Message-ID: <01D04F840CF1D111817100A0C9C9BA7406744B@GSSERVER>
From: Bob <bob_jones@isp.co.uk>
To: John <john@reeftours.co.au>
Subject: Happy Birthday John!
Date: Mon, 27 Mar 2000 09:44:35 -0900
X-Priority: 3
MIME-Version: 1.0
X-Mailer: Internet Mail Service (5.0.1459.44)
Content-Type: text/plain;
        charset="iso-8859-1"
Content-Transfer-Encoding: quoted-printable
```

Figure 32: Example of message header (received message)

Here you can see the way in which the message was routed. It is easy to see at what point the message arrives in Australia: notice the difference in the lines describing date and time. Once the message has been routed from Bob's server, instead of +0100, the time appears as +1000. This is the time zone for the receiving server in Australia, 10 hours ahead of GMT and 9 hours ahead of Bob.

Don't be put off by all the technical information in these files. I'm not going to explain it: there's little point as it is rarely necessary to understand it. In 12 years of using e-mail in its various stages of development, I have only once needed to look at an e-mail header – and then only to prove what time a message was sent and received. In the unlikely event that you are asked to check a mail header, most probably in a work situation, there is bound to be a more technically aware person to help you out. If you really need to know what a particular term means, try one of the Internet encyclopaedias listed in the appendix *Useful Internet addresses.*

International e-mail considerations

There are two main considerations when you are sending and receiving mail from other countries:

* The difference in language, which might require translation services.

* The difference in typed characters, which might require you to change your encoding setting.

Translating e-mail

If you are likely to correspond by e-mail with people who do not have English as their native language, you might occasionally require messages to be translated. In addition to the human translator or translation bureaux there are now many computerised translation products available, some of which are provided free on the Internet. Whether these will be of use will primarily depend on the type of information contained in your messages. If it is specific to a product, technology or industrial process in which many non-standard words are used, you are probably wasting your time with automated translations. If, however, the information is of a basic nature, it might be worth considering. If you are in business and require basic translation of more than just e-mail, computerised translation could provide some of the services you require, but be warned: it will rarely provide a word-perfect version that reads like a native document.

Getting the best from computerised translation

If you need to translate an e-mail message from English into another language, you should make sure the message is written correctly to allow the clearest possible translation. Translation software can do a good job, but it requires more thought on the part of the user than some people imagine: remember that machines do not have the reasoning capabilities of humans. Producing good machine translation text is identical to producing text that humans can read easily without extra effort.

Here are some tips:

- Write your documents in standard, formal English, not conversational language.

- Write clearly and explicitly: avoid ambiguity, unclear references, colloquialisms and slang.

- Use simple, clear sentences, even if this sounds a little stilted in English.

- Use proper grammar and do not omit words, even if it is acceptable to do so in English.

- Make headings and other non-sentence items, such as list points, very obvious.

- Avoid idiomatic expressions.

- Use possessive apostrophes only. Avoid contractions such as don't or won't.

- Do not split compound verbs.

- Use accents correctly.

- Use line breaks only at the end of sentences.

- Update the dictionary to include any unfamiliar words.

- Proofread before you translate.

- Check context when translating interactively.

Translation services on the Internet

Some service providers and websites offer free online translation of small documents, with the option to refer the document to a human translator for checking (for which a fee is required). Such systems have not yet been available for long enough for a reasoned judgement to be made on how effective they are compared with the more traditional translation options. The addresses of some websites that offer such services are provided in the appendix *Useful Internet addresses*.

Changing the encoding for a message

If you receive a message from another e-mail user in a country that uses a different alphabet, you might need to change the encoding of that message to be able to view it correctly. This particularly applies to postings from newsgroups and lists, where the message header may be incomplete and thus not show the encoding used by the sender. You should not need to change the encoding when you reply to a message: it automatically adopts the encoding of the original message. You might need to set different encoding when writing a new message to someone whose alphabet you know to be different.

The options supported by most e-mail software include Latin, Western European or Central European (usable for most English-speaking countries); Greek; Turkish; Cyrillic (Russian); Japanese (Kanji), Chinese (often more than one version); Korean; and an option called Unicode, which in theory is acceptable by all computers, although some browsers do not recognise it.

If it is likely that most of your e-mail correspondence will be with one of the countries represented above, it might be worth changing the default encoding setting. To change the default for all messages in Microsoft® Outlook Express, go to the main window and select **Options** from the **Tools** menus. Select the **Send** page and click on **International settings** to select the language you require. To change the encoding setting for a single message, select **Encoding** from the **Format** menu of the message window. If you cannot find the encoding setting you require, you can usually obtain further definitions from the website that supports your e-mail or browser software.

Some e-mail software also uses the term 'encode' to mean the format used for sending the message (names of these codes include MIME and UUENCODE). This is generally subject to the limitations of your software and is not related to language.

Legal considerations

The legal status of e-mail is as yet undetermined in some countries, although this is likely to change as it becomes more widely used as the standard method of business communication. In many countries, e-mail messages are submissible as evidence in many of the types of case that could be brought before a court: in both the US and UK it has been used by one side or the other in cases involving discrimination, libel, fraud and unfair dismissal. For example, in the American case of Strauss vs Microsoft Corp in 1995, e-mail messages between

Microsoft® employees were considered admissible evidence in a sexual discrimination lawsuit.

The problem with e-mail as evidence lies in the insecure nature of electronic communication. Unless a message has been digitally signed, it is not possible to say for certain that it was written and sent by a particular individual: it could have been sent by anyone who had access to that person's e-mail address and password. In a recent case in the UK, a worker was convicted of sending racially offensive e-mail to others within the organisation using a colleague's e-mail address. It took a great deal of surveillance to track down the culprit, after the apparent sender proved he could not have sent the messages at the time they were despatched, and a great deal of evidence was required in order to gain a conviction.

Digital certificates do offer a more secure method of communication, with a virtual guarantee that the message was actually sent by the signatory, and thus are accepted in many countries as the equivalent of an ink signature on paper. E-mail messages that are digitally signed therefore are to be considered the same as any other contract: if you promise something in a digitally signed e-mail, you must deliver. If you offer someone a job by e-mail using a digital certificate, you must honour that offer and follow the legal processes related to employment law. It does not necessarily follow that without a digital signature you are not legally bound: it depends on the circumstances and the content of the message, but it could well be less easy to enforce.

If you correspond internationally by e-mail, it is well worth finding out the legal status of e-mail in the countries with which you correspond. After all, it is no security that your message is considered a legal contract in the UK if it is not considered as such in the country in which the recipient is based.

In general, whatever the current legal position, it is wise to remember that because e-mail leaves an electronic trail, it creates a vast amount of easily traceable information. As such, and especially if it is the only source of such information, it could possibly be subject to subpoena for use at trial in the case of any dispute, so you should always take care never to state something in an e-mail that could be used against you. Remember, e-mail is neither private nor secure, so it can be easy to get caught out.

Changing your e-mail address

If you are happy with your service provider, you may never need to change your e-mail address. Even if you move house, you need only change your dialling settings to continue. However, if you find a better deal, your provider closes down, or you are moving to another country, you may need to change to a new e-mail address. Before you do so, check the following:

• The notice period required by your service provider for you to close your account, usually one month.

• Whether you will be required to continue payments, for example, if you signed up for a minimum 12-month term.

• Whether your current ISP will forward mail to a new account with another ISP, and for how long; how they will deal with messages sent to your old account once this period has run out.

• Whether you can save your stored e-mail and items such as your address book details to a portable format, so you can use them with another account.

When you have this information, you can plan your change to create the minimum disruption. Plan ahead to give yourself time to look into the various deals on offer from ISPs, as well as new e-mail software if you want to upgrade to a more recent version.

Signing up to a new service provider is easy: just install the software from a CD-ROM or Internet site and create the e-mail address you require, as you probably did with your previous service provider. Before removing your old ISP software, send a message to everyone in your address book, telling them of your new address and the date from which it will be effective. Amend your usual message signature to include details of your change of e-mail address; if your printed stationery shows your e-mail address, change this too. If possible, operate both accounts for a few days at least to ease the changeover. (Your e-mail software will allow you to dial in to more than one ISP, although you may have to connect twice to do so.) During this time, if you are also changing your e-mail software, transfer the contents of your old mailbox to your new account, including any file management structure; your old address book to the new one; and if necessary, set up any options in the new software to mirror your existing display.

If you use newsgroups, bulletin boards or lists as a subscribed member, you will need to re-subscribe using your new e-mail address. You should also unsubscribe using the old e-mail address before it is removed, otherwise the newsgroup/list server will continue sending to the old address as well. Although this is unlikely to affect you, it will result in returned messages from the old ISP to the server, and this only adds to the traffic that slows the Internet further.

Abbreviations and codes

Abbreviations abound in the world of computers and the Internet, as you would expect from something originally designed for the military and developed by computer programmers. This appendix explains a few of them, and also looks at the emoticons often used in personal mail or newsgroup postings. If you can't find what you are looking for, use one of the Internet encyclopaedias recommended in the appendix *Useful Internet addresses*.

Abbreviations and acronyms used in e-mail

Abbreviations are frequently used in e-mail, especially by technical people or in newsgroup, forum or chatroom postings. They can save a lot of typing but only if the recipient understands what they mean, and many are unsuitable for use in a business document. If you are working in a specific field of business such as chemicals, IT or printing, you may find abbreviations are used to describe aspects of your work – these of course are not restricted to use in e-mail.

Here are some of those most commonly used. If you receive mail containing others that you do not understand, just ask the sender to explain or check. Alternatively, check the abbreviations listed in one of the other Internet encyclopaedias shown in the next appendix.

Most users type abbreviations describing emotions or facial expressions within < >, for example, <BG> for 'big grin'. (These abbreviations are often replaceable with an emoticon, as described later in this appendix.) You don't need to use these symbols around the other abbreviations shown in this list.

Abbreviation	**Meaning**
ADN	Any day now
AFAIK	As far as I know
AFK	Away from keyboard
A/S/L?	Age/sex/location?
B4N or BFN	Bye for now
BAK	Back at the keyboard
BBL	Be back later
<BG>	Big grin
BRB	Be right back
BTA	But then again ...
BTW	By the way
BWDIK	But what do I know?
CU	See you
CUL	See you later
CYO	See you online
DIKU	Do I know you?
DQMOT	Don't quote me on this
<EG>	Evil grin
EMFBI	Excuse me for butting in
EOM	End of message
EOT	End of thread (used only in newsgroups, chatrooms and BBS)
F2F	Face to face
FAQ	Frequently-asked question(s)
FLA	Four-letter acronym
FWIW	For what it's worth
FYI	For your information
<G>	Grin
GA	Go ahead
GMTA	Great minds think alike
GTRM	Going to read mail
HAND	Have a nice day
HTH	Hope this helps
IAC	In any case
IC	I see
IIRC	If I recall/remember/recollect correctly
ILU or ILY	I love you
IM	Immediate message
IMHO	In my humble opinion
IMO	In my opinion

IOW	In other words
IRL	In real life
IYSWIM	If you see what I mean
JIC	Just in case
JK	Just kidding
KWIM?	Know what I mean?
L8R	Later
<LOL>	Laughing out loud
<LTM>	Laugh to myself
LTNS	Long time no see
NFW	No feasible way
NP or N/P	No problem
NRN	No response necessary
OIC	Oh, I see
OTOH	On the other hand
OTTOMH	Off the top of my head
PMFJIB	Pardon me for jumping in, but ...
RL	Real life
RPG	Role-playing games
RSN	Real soon now
RTFM	Read the flippin' manual
SO	Significant other
STW	Search the web
TAFN	That's all for now
THX or TU	Thanks/thank you
TIA	Thanks in advance
TLA	Three-letter acronym
TLK2UL8R or TTYL	Talk to you later
TMI	Too much information
TTFN	Ta-ta for now
UW	You're welcome
WFM	Works for me
WIBNI	Wouldn't it be nice if
WTGP?	Want to go private? ('private' means writing e-mail directly to one another rather than via the newsgroup or forum)
WU?	What's up?
WUF?	Where are you from?
WYSIWYG	What you see is what you get

Emoticons

Emoticons are little pictures created from punctuation. Sometimes they are called 'smileys' because when you see them on the screen at a certain angle they look like faces. Their purpose is to express emotion or intent, for example, happiness, sadness, anger or frustration, and thereby overcome the problem of the lack of face-to-face contact. While they are generally unsuitable for business communication, they are frequently used in more personal e-mail and on bulletin board postings, so it is worth listing the common ones here.

The most basic 'smileys' are so commonly used that some software automatically detects when you type this series of characters and changes it into a 'proper smiley', as shown below.

Happy	:) or :-) or ☺
Sad	:(or :-(or ☹
Only joking! (a wink)	;) or ;-)
Bored	:0 or :-0
Angry or annoyed	:-|| or :-<
Crying	:'-(
Really happy	:-)) or :-D
Kiss	:-*
Surprised	:-o
Grim	:-|
Perplexed	:-/
Tongue-in-cheek	;-^)

These are fairly well-established, but of course there are many more and new ones come into being on an almost daily basis, but if you use a new one, your recipient might not understand it. If you receive one that you don't understand, ask the sender or a computer geek!

There are several lists of emoticons available on the Internet: a particularly definitive list can be downloaded from www.utopiasw.demon.co.uk/emoticon.html

Alternatively, try one of the encyclopaedia listed in the next appendix, or just search on 'smiley' or 'emoticon'. For an extensive list of more than 650 emoticons, read *Smileys* by David Sanderson (O'Reilly & Associations, Inc, ISBN 1-56592-041-4).

Abbreviations in Internet and e-mail addresses

There are several conventions for addresses, to designate the type of organisation and/or the country in which it is based. Some of the most common are shown below with the relevant part highlighted in italic. A full list can be found in most of the Internet encyclopaedia sites, such as www.whatis.com

Address	Meaning
user@alk.*net*	A network
user@charity.*org*	A non-profit organisation
user@dti.*gov*.uk	A government department
user@isp.*com*	A commercial company or service provider
user@nuke.*mil*	A military site
user@test.*co*.uk	A commercial company or division for a particular country (in this case based in the UK; see below for further country codes)
user@universe.*int*	An international organisation
user@wsthan.*edu*	An education provider; school or university

Country codes

Country codes may be appended to the end of some e-mail and Internet addresses, showing the country in which the organisation or individual is based. This is most common with .co, .gov, and .org addresses, which tend to be country-specific; most .com and .net addresses have no country suffix. Some American addresses show the state abbreviation rather than a country code.

All country codes are determined by the International Standards Organisation (ISO). A full list of country codes can be found on the Internet by searching on the terms 'diagraph' or 'country code', or by application to your country's standards organisation.

Some of the most commonly used abbreviations are shown overleaf.

Country code	Country
at	Austria
au	Australia
be	Belgium
ca	Canada
ch	Switzerland
cn	China
cz	The Czech Republic
de	Germany
dk	Denmark
es	Spain
fr	France
hk	Hong Kong
hu	Hungary
ie	Ireland
in	India
it	Italy
jp	Japan
nl	Netherlands (Holland)
no	Norway
nz	New Zealand
pt	Portugal
ru	The Russian Federation
se	Sweden
sg	Singapore
uk	UK
us	USA
za	South Africa

Useful Internet addresses

This appendix lists some website addresses that you might find useful. There are many others of course, and it is not the intention of the author to suggest that these are the best or only solutions available. Note that website addresses are subject to change without notice, so you might find that some of these are no longer available. If so, run an Internet search with the country name and the heading as the search parameters and this should display a current list of suitable alternatives.

ISP websites

Most of these offer free connection software, some make a charge. Some are lists of ISPs provided by third parties, others are the ISPs' own websites.

A good world-wide listing of ISPs is available at www.thedirectory.org

UK and Ireland
A review of all the current UK providers can be found at: www.ispreview.co.uk
The following are ISP sites:

www.freeserve.co.uk
www.btclick.com
www.aol.com
www.virgin.net
www.iol.com (Ireland only)

Australia
A list of ISPs can be found at http://aaa.com.au/online/isp
Otherwise try:

www.ozemail.com.au
www.bigpond.com
www.dingoblue.com.au
http://surfbroad.alphalink.com.au

New Zealand
www.surf4nix.com
www.wiredkiwis.co.nz/isps
www.thenet.co.nz
www.voyager.co.nz

South Africa
A list of ISPs is available at http://isp-help.hypermart.net
Otherwise try:
www.global.net.za
www.saol.com

Free e-mail websites

World-wide
www.hotmail.com
www.mailcity.com

UK only
www.talk21.com

Australia only
www.goconnect.com.au

E-mail directories

Most ISPs provide one of these, usually showing their own subscribers only. Some others include:
www.infospace.com
www.whowhere.lycos.com
http://people.yahoo.com
http://members@netscape.com
www.192.com (UK only)

Zip or compression products

WinZip is usually supplied as part of Microsoft® Windows®.
PKzip's homepage is at www.pkware.com

Pkzip for DOS is also available for download at
ftp://ftp.demon.co.uk/pub/ibmpc/dos/apps/zip/pkz204g.exe
and WinZip for Windows® is available for download at:
ftp://ftp.demon.co.uk/pub/ibmpc/win3/apps/zip/winzip/winzi
p56.exe

Virus detection

There are many products available, so shop around. The
following have been recommended in the computer press:

www.trend.com/pc-cillin
www.symantec.com/nav
www.housecall.antivirus.com/housecall
www.metro.ch/avpve

The following sites offer information on viruses:

www.virusdatabase.com
www.avp.ch/avpve

Online technical dictionaries and encyclopaedias

www.whatis.com
www.webopedia.internet.com
http://techweb.com/encyclopedia
www.netlingo.com

Online translation

www.systransoft.com
http://babelfish.altavista.digital.com (note: no www)
http://freetranslation.com

Lists of bulletin boards (BBS)

www.boardwatch.com
http://bbslist.rgcomputing.com
www.bestweb.net/~ecw/excal/
www.thedirectory.org/diamond/bbslists.htm

Subscription and discussion lists

www.liszt.com
www.lsoft.com/lists/listref.html
www.reference.com

Chatrooms

www.irc.net
www.irchelp.org

Emoticons

www.utopiasw.demon.co.uk/emoticon.html
http://lakeonline.com/internut.emot.htm
www.robelle.com/smugbook/smiley.html

Digital certificates

World-wide
www.thawte.com
www.verisign.com
www.netsign.com

UK and Ireland
www.trustwise.com
www.trust365.com

Europe
www.globalsign.net

Australia
www.esign.com.au

South Africa
www.saca.net

Alternative names for e-mail functions

Throughout this book, examples and guidance are given using Microsoft® Outlook Express software. The list below shows the names of the corresponding function or feature name in other commonly-used e-mail software, which you can use to find the appropriate section in your product manual. If the term you are looking for does not appear in the list, it is probably the same for all the listed products. If the product you use does not appear in this list, use some of the terms shown here to help identify the function in the index of your product's manual or online help. If it does not appear, it may not be a supported function of your product.

A dash in the table indicates that this feature does not appear in the tested version of the software: it might appear in other versions of the same product, especially more recent editions.

Microsoft® Outlook Express	Netscape® Messenger™	Qualcomm® Eudora®	MSN™ Hotmail®
Inbox	Inbox	In mailbox	Inbox
Outbox	Outbox	Out mailbox	–
Sent items	Sent	Sent items	Sent messages
Deleted items	Trash	Trash	Trashcan
New mail	To: mail	New message	Compose
Receive all	Get mail	Check mail	–
Send all	Send messages in outbox	Send queued messages	–
Message rules	–	Filters	Filters
Folder	Folder	Mailbox	Folder
Options	Preferences	Options	Options
Show header	Show headers	Blah Blah Blah	Message Headers*

Microsoft® Outlook Express	Netscape® Messenger™	Qualcomm® Eudora®	MSN™ Hotmail®
Group by conversation	Thread messages	Group by subject	Sort by subject†
Move to folder	Move	Transfer	Move to
User name	Name	Personality	Sign-in name
Word wrap	Wrap long lines	Word wrap	Line width*
Text settings (for replies and forwards)	Automatically quote …	Replying options	Replying to messages

* All these Hotmail® options are found in the **Preferences** section of the **Options** page.

† This is not true 'threading' as threads are not collapsible, but it does sort by the message subject.

Glossary

The following terms are either used in this book, or are in common use in e-mail or Internet discussions. If you are unsure of other terms, try checking one of the Internet dictionaries listed on page 129.

account   Your account with an ISP may comprise one or more e-mail addresses and other information that allows you to access the Internet.

attachment   A file that is sent with an e-mail.

bookmarks   A browser function that allows you to store details of the pages on the web that you like and to which you want to return. Some applications, including Microsoft® Internet Explorer, call these Favourites.

bulletin board or BBS   An Internet 'meeting place', where you can post messages and read messages from others on a specific topic. Similar to a **newsgroup** but less interactive.

compression   Reducing the size of a file through the use of a zip or compression utility program. This helps to speed the file through the network, and makes it quicker to upload and download. See page 81 for more detail.

cookie   A text file used by websites to keep a record of visitors. When you visit a site a cookie is stored on your hard drive so the site recognises you when you return, saving you the need to retype. The cookie also tells a site the names of the last few sites you visited and what type of browser you are using. It can result in unwanted e-mail (*see* **spam**). If it worries you, you can instruct your browser not to accept cookies. Check your manual for the procedure.

corrupted file   A file that has been damaged. Corruption can occur through splitting, virus attack, or incompatibility with software. There are some utilities on offer to fix corrupted files, but not all forms of corruption are fixable. It is usually best to request the file again.

crash The name usually given to a software failure that results in one or more computers being shut down. If you use a computer, you are probably familiar with the signs: your keyboard or mouse no longer respond to commands, and the screen appears to be locked up. The same occurs with servers, and in most cases it is caused by an overload of information on the system. Web servers often crash if they get an excessive amount of people trying to access them at once. Generally the only way to resolve a crash is to shut down the machine and restart it.

cybercafé A public facility, usually a coffee shop or wine bar, where PCs are provided from which anyone may access the Internet. There is usually a small fee to cover costs, and you might need to book in advance, particularly for live netcasts of popular events.

digital certificate A security device that allows two people to exchange e-mail in a relatively secure manner and which is recognised as the legal equivalent of a written signature in many parts of the world. This function is not supported by all software, so consult your manual for details. See *Getting a digital certificate* on page 111 for more details.

domain The part of an e-mail address that shows the name of the company or service provider. See also page 37.

e-commerce The trading and promotion of goods and services on the Internet: basically, commerce on the web.

electronic signature Personal details, usually in plain text form, which you can attach to your e-mail messages. See the section *Signing your messages* on page 55 for details and an example.

emoticons This is the proper name for the 'smileys' that sometimes appear on e-mail messages. See *Emoticons* on page 124 for details.

encryption The coding of a file or message to prevent interception by non-authorised persons. Encryption generally follows a cipher-style format, with both parties having the relevant decoding mechanism.

FTP   File Transfer Protocol, a mechanism by which files are loaded to, downloaded from and managed on web servers or other network services. See the section *Using FTP to send files* on page 104.

filter   See **rules**

firewall   A secure 'layer' around a company's intranet or other network that prevents unauthorised persons from outside the company, such as hackers, from gaining access to company information. It may also be used to prevent information from leaving the company's network from the inside.

folder   Sometimes called mailbox, and used to store messages outside the inbox. For details of how to create and use folders, see *Setting up a filing system* on page 58.

forum/fora   A discussion group/groups, often technical, operated by a newsgroup, BBS or list. Members air their views on topics and questions submitted by other members of the forum.

freeware   Programs or other software that is made available by its owners free of charge, for anyone to use for as long as they like. Utility programs and graphics are often available as freeware on the Internet. Contrast with **shareware**.

gateway   A server at the entry or exit point for a company or service provider. When an e-mail message is routed from one country or company to another, it passes through several gateways, each of which analyses the address information and routes the message accordingly.

global village   The term often used to describe the effect of the Internet, and electronic communication in general, on social and business communication. In effect, with the advent of free or cheap e-mail, you can talk to anyone as if they lived next door, rather than halfway around the world, time zones permitting, of course.

hacker   A person who invades computer systems to obtain information, often of a personal or confidential nature. Some large companies employ 'professional' hackers to establish the security of their systems. Hackers are often responsible for the leaking of security information to the media, and usually operate from home. Using sophisticated telephony and computer equipment, they dial into systems and automatically generate user name and password information until they get the right combination and the system allows them access. For this reason, you should never use obvious passwords, such as your name, birthday or address, or those of your partner or children. Use something like your favourite colour, that others are less able to find out.

header This is the part of an e-mail message that contains technical information such as routing, server codes and language/encoding details. See *The message header* on page 113 for more information.

HTML Hypertext Mark-up Language. A system of codes that produces formatted text and graphics, which is used to generate documents for the Internet and can be used to format e-mail messages. Most e-mail software now allows you to write messages in HTML without requiring any knowledge of the codes, but some e-mail software on older systems is unable to display HTML and will show it only as plain text.

hyperlink A highlighted word or phrase in an internet or e-mail document that, when clicked on, takes you directly to the document it references. Often used in e-mail to direct the reader to a particular website.

inline When describing graphics or other attachments, *inline* means that they appear within the message, not as a file that you have to open separately. Usually items appear inline only if your software can view HTML.

Internet Service Provider (ISP) A company that provides you with software to connect to the Internet, and thus use e-mail. See *Choosing a service provider* on page 30 for more details.

intranet An Internet-like structure that is available only to certain users; usually within a company or other organisation. Items are accessed and stored as if they were on the Internet, but the general public cannot gain access to them.

ISDN Integrated Services Digital Network is an international standard for transmitting and receiving voice, images and data over telephone lines (whether digital or standard). Most ISDN lines actually give you two lines at once, allowing you to use one for voice calls and the other for data. Alternatively you can use both for data to give you a faster response – up to three times faster than the fastest modems.

log in If working on an intranet, this refers to the point at which you have to supply your user name and password to connect to the network. If working from home or a non-networked computer, this is the point at which you dial in to the ISP to connect to the Internet or send and receive messages. It usually requires you to enter your user name or e-mail address and a password.

log out or log off The point at which you end connection to the network; for an intranet, when you select the option to exit or disconnect; for a non-networked PC, when you select Disconnect to end the phone connection.

NC Network computer. A simple terminal that allows access to the Internet or another network. See *The next big thing* on page 33.

netcast A broadcast made over the Internet – online TV, if you like. Often used for live broadcast of sporting and political events.

nickname A name you specify when adding a person to your address book that allows you to send mail to them simply by typing this name. This saves the need to remember all or part of an e-mail address.

online service provider A service provider that operates from an internet website, allowing you to connect and send or receive mail from any internet-enabled computer. MSN™ Hotmail® is one example. Sometimes called an OSP.

portal A website that offers services: for example, matching jobs to qualified experts or sellers to buyers. Revenue usually comes from advertising on the site: you should not be charged for an entry.

posting An e-mail message sent to a newsgroup or bulletin board, to be posted on its list or sent to its subscribers.

properties The settings used by your software, or the settings and characteristics of a message. The former are sometimes called Preferences or Options.

rules Values you set that identify messages and perform a set task on them, such as redirecting messages to a particular folder or returning them to the sender. Sometimes called filters.

search engine A program that you use to find Internet sites by entering one or more keywords. The program searches listed sites for the keywords, indexes the results and displays them on your screen. Without search engines, it would be almost impossible to find what you wanted on the Internet, unless you had a specific **URL**.

secure message A message that has been encoded, and encrypted, to avoid interference from hackers, often with a digital certificate.

server A computer on which files are stored or through which files and e-mail are transmitted. Your ISP operates a server for your incoming and outgoing mail, and one or more to host (store) website pages and search engines. All your Internet and e-mail activities are routed through a server.

shareware Programs and products that are made available free on the basis of trust: once you have become familiar with them, you are required to pay to continue using them. Contrast with **freeware**.

signature file See **electronic signature**.

spam Unwanted or junk e-mail. Like most junk mail, you are left wondering how the sender got hold of your name. The answer, as shown above, is through cookies. Some spam results from other sources, in much the same way as junk mail, fax or telephone calls, but this is generally less common. See **cookies**.

surfing Using the internet, or, to be exact, the world-wide web. It is called 'surfing' because it is supposed to be quick and effortless!

tags The name for the technical bits of HTML that tell the computer how to display it. They are usually enclosed in chevrons, like this: <BODY>.

threading Grouping messages by topic or conversation. This is often used when viewing newsgroups and other multi-user information, to sort the relevant from the irrelevant. See the section *Setting display options* on page 72 for details of how to thread your mail.

URL Uniform Resource Locator: the official name for an Internet address. For example, the URL of Webopedia is www.webopedia.com

virus A destructive command or program that causes damage to the software on your computer, usually by changing or deleting files or causing commands to repeat indefinitely. See also **worm**. For further details see *Avoiding computer viruses* on page 47.

WAP Wireless Application Protocol. A new technology that allows access to the Internet from portable, non-wired equipment. See *The next big thing* on page 33 for details.

webpage One online page of a website. The main webpage is called the homepage.

website A collection of webpages that provide information, usually on the owner of the website, and might allow online trading (e-commerce), enquiries, or other facilities.

world-wide web (www) The international network of computers providing information to others via the Internet. It is called a 'web' because each item, or page, generally provides links to other pages provided by other companies or individuals, and in theory, it should be possible to find almost any website purely by following enough links (although of course it is quicker to use a search facility!).

worm A particularly damaging type of **virus**. See also page 47.

zip file See **compression**.

Index